OS X Mountain Lion
Pocket Guide

Chris Seibold

O'REILLY®

Beijing · Cambridge · Farnham · Köln · Sebastopol · Tokyo

OS X Mountain Lion Pocket Guide
by Chris Seibold

Copyright © 2012 Chris Seibold. All rights reserved.
Printed in the United States of America.

Published by O'Reilly Media, Inc., 1005 Gravenstein Highway North, Sebastopol, CA 95472.

O'Reilly books may be purchased for educational, business, or sales promotional use. Online editions are also available for most titles (*http://my.safari booksonline.com*). For more information, contact our corporate/institutional sales department: 800-998-9938 or *corporate@oreilly.com*.

Editor: Dawn Mann
Production Editor: Melanie Yarbrough
Proofreader: Julie Van Keuren
Indexer: Kevin Broccoli
Cover Designer: Karen Montgomery
Interior Designer: David Futato
Illustrator: Robert Romano

July 2012:   First Edition.

Revision History for the First Edition:
    2012-07-11   First release
    2012-08-10   Second release
    2012-10-05   Third release

See *http://oreilly.com/catalog/errata.csp?isbn=9781449330323* for release details.

Nutshell Handbook, the Nutshell Handbook logo, and the O'Reilly logo are registered trademarks of O'Reilly Media, Inc. *OS X Mountain Lion Pocket Guide*, the image of a puma, and related trade dress are trademarks of O'Reilly Media, Inc.

Many of the designations used by manufacturers and sellers to distinguish their products are claimed as trademarks. Where those designations appear in this book, and O'Reilly Media, Inc., was aware of a trademark claim, the designations have been printed in caps or initial caps.

While every precaution has been taken in the preparation of this book, the publisher and authors assume no responsibility for errors or omissions, or for damages resulting from the use of the information contained herein.

ISBN: 978-1-449-33032-3

[M]

1348864976

Contents

Preface

OS X was first released to the public over a decade ago as Mac OS X Beta (code-named Kodiak). The decade after that saw Mac OS X go from an interesting oddity unsuited to daily work to a usable operating system with little third-party support to everything most people want out of an operating system and a little more.

Technology doesn't stand still, and the days of being tied to a desk if you wanted to use your Mac (as most people were when OS X was first revealed) are long gone. Apple now offers lots of ways to use Apple technology. You've got Macs, of course, but you also have Apple TVs, iPods, iPhones, and iPads. People want to use *all* those things, and that's where Mountain Lion shines. Apple says Mountain Lion is "Inspired by iPad," and it offers a stunning number of new features designed to make working with multiple devices easier and more streamlined. Mountain Lion does the obvious things—like putting documents in iCloud and sharing your screen with your Apple TV —as well as some unexpected things like making Twitter available system-wide.

Like Reminders on your iPhone? Love notifications on your iPad? Then you're going to really enjoy Mountain Lion. Apps that were available only on iOS devices are now an integral part of OS X. Other apps were renamed and reworked to match their iOS counterparts: iChat is now Messages, and iCal is now Calendar, to cite two examples.

You'll also be relieved to know that the cost of all the improvements and new features that comprise Mountain Lion isn't increasing. In fact, the price of the update actually *dropped* $10.00 to $19.99. And since you can get it only from the App Store, you don't even have to get off your couch to upgrade!

NOTE

This book focuses on what you'd see onscreen if you bought a brand-new Mac with Mountain Lion on it. If you upgrade from Lion to Mountain Lion, some things you see may be slightly different, because some settings will get transferred over from Lion. This book tries to point out such instances whenever applicable, but you may spot differences not noted here.

Conventions Used in This Book

The following typographical conventions are used in this book:

Italic

    Indicates new terms, URLs, email addresses, filenames, and file extensions.

`Constant width`

    Used for program listings, as well as within paragraphs to refer to program elements such as variable or function names, databases, data types, environment variables, statements, and keywords.

`Constant width bold`

    Shows commands or other text that should be typed literally by the user.

`Constant width italic`

    Shows text that should be replaced with user-supplied values or by values determined by context.

Menu Symbols

With this Pocket Guide, you'll always know which button to press. The key labeled "option" is called Option throughout this book. The key with the clover symbol (officially called the Place of Interest symbol) is represented by ⌘, which looks precisely like the symbol on the keyboard.

Apple itself uses some symbols for these keys that you won't see on your keyboard. If you click the menu bar, you'll see symbols next to some commands that indicate their keyboard shortcuts. For example, if you click the File menu while running TextEdit, you'll see a long sequence of symbols for the "Show Properties" shortcut, as shown in Figure P-1.

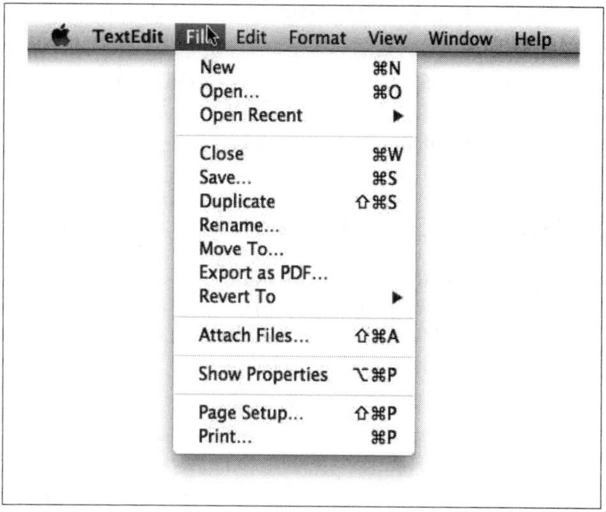

Figure P-1. Keyboard shortcuts in TextEdit's File menu

From left to right, the symbols are Option (⌥), Command (⌘), and P. This indicates that you need to hold down the Option and ⌘ keys while pressing P. In this book, you'll see this written as "Option-⌘-P" instead.

A less commonly used modifier is the Control key, which Apple indicates with the ∧ symbol; this book spells it out as "Control." You may also encounter ℧, which indicates the Esc key.

The symbol for the Eject button (⏏) is the same as the symbol silk-screened onto most Apple keyboards. The Delete key is symbolized with ⌫.

Attribution and Permissions

This book is here to help you get your job done. If you reference limited parts of it in your work or writings, we appreciate, but don't require, attribution. An attribution usually includes the title, author, publisher, and ISBN, like so: "*OS X Mountain Lion Pocket Guide*, by Chris Seibold (O'Reilly). Copyright 2012 Chris Seibold, 978-1-449-33032-3."

If you feel your use of examples or quotations from this book falls outside fair use or the permission given above, feel free to contact us at *permissions@oreilly.com*.

Safari® Books Online

Safari Books Online (*www.safaribookson line.com*) is an on-demand digital library that delivers expert content in both book and video form from the world's leading authors in technology and business.

Technology professionals, software developers, web designers, and business and creative professionals use Safari Books Online as their primary resource for research, problem solving, learning, and certification training.

Safari Books Online offers a range of product mixes and pricing programs for organizations, government agencies, and individuals. Subscribers have access to thousands of books, training videos, and prepublication manuscripts in one fully searchable database from publishers like O'Reilly Media, Prentice

Hall Professional, Addison-Wesley Professional, Microsoft Press, Sams, Que, Peachpit Press, Focal Press, Cisco Press, John Wiley & Sons, Syngress, Morgan Kaufmann, IBM Redbooks, Packt, Adobe Press, FT Press, Apress, Manning, New Riders, McGraw-Hill, Jones & Bartlett, Course Technology, and dozens more. For more information about Safari Books Online, please visit us online.

How to Contact Us

Please address comments and questions concerning this book to the publisher:

O'Reilly Media, Inc.
1005 Gravenstein Highway North
Sebastopol, CA 95472
800-998-9938 (in the United States or Canada)
707-829-0515 (international or local)
707-829-0104 (fax)

We have a web page for this book, where we list errata, examples, and any additional information. You can access this page at:

http://bit.ly/osx_mountain_lion_pg

To comment or ask technical questions about this book, send email to:

bookquestions@oreilly.com

For more information about our books, courses, conferences, and news, see our website at *http://www.oreilly.com.*

Find us on Facebook: *http://facebook.com/oreilly*

Follow us on Twitter: *http://twitter.com/oreillymedia*

Watch us on YouTube: *http://www.youtube.com/oreillymedia*

Acknowledgments

I'd like to thank Dawn Mann for turning this into a readable book and Bakari Chavanu for making sure the tech stuff was correct. Thanks to Brian Jepson for teaching me so much and Hadley Stern for getting me involved in writing books. And finally, thanks to Yan Hong for watching Nathaniel while I was banging away at the keyboard.

CHAPTER 1

What's New in Mountain Lion?

Apple touts OS X Mountain Lion as "inspired by the iPad," and once you start using Mountain Lion, you'll soon agree. But even though iOS (the operating system behind the iPad, iPhone, and iPod touch) has clearly influenced OS X Mountain Lion, OS X is still a distinct operating system made specifically for the Mac and not just a half-baked clone of iOS. But noting that doesn't tell you what you're interested in: What's new in OS X Mountain Lion?

According to Apple, Mountain Lion has over 200 new features. That's a nice round number, but you're probably more interested in learning about the most *useful* new features, the big changes, and what to expect when you switch to Mountain Lion. In that case, then, the following rundown of major new features is for you.

Improved iCloud Integration

iCloud, which Apple released in June 2011, replaced MobileMe and was, happily, free of charge. In Mountain Lion, iCloud plays a more significant role than it did in Lion. More apps can sync using iCloud, and setting it up is simply a matter of typing in your iCloud password.

NOTE

Apple now calls all programs "apps," whether they're on a Mac, iPad, iPhone, or iPod. This book uses the terms "app," "program," and "application" interchangeably.

What can you sync with iCloud? The usual suspects and more: Mail, Contacts, Calendars, FaceTime, Notes, Reminders, Game Center, App Store, Documents, Safari bookmarks, and even open *tabs* in Safari. It's pretty amazing to use FaceTime or Safari on one Mac and then grab your iPad and find the same FaceTime conversation—or the same open tabs—there. All this integration means that starting a task on one of your devices doesn't mean you have to finish that task on the same device—you're free to jump from Mac to iPad to iPhone and back.

NOTE

There's a lot of great integration between your Apple devices now, but when iOS 6 comes out in the fall of 2012, there will be even more integration—and Mountain Lion will be up to the task.

Setting up iCloud is, in true Apple style, extremely easy. When you install Mountain Lion, you'll be prompted to enter your iCloud login info. (No iCloud account? No problem, you can set one up anytime by opening up the iCloud preference pane [see "iCloud" on page 147] or visiting *www.icloud.com*.) Once you've done so, all the data you want shared between your devices gets synced automatically.

It's easy to overlook one key benefit of iCloud in Mountain Lion: easy collaboration. For example, if you've shared a Pages document (see "Documents & Data" on page 150), any changes that anyone makes to it get reflected in all the copies of the document *immediately*. It's a great feature for group projects.

NOTE

If you're used to Google Docs, the idea of saving documents online is familiar. But unlike with Google Docs, you *don't* have to be online to work on your iCloud documents.

At this point you'd probably like a comprehensive list of apps that work with iCloud. That, sadly, isn't possible because iCloud integration isn't strictly for Apple apps: third-party developers can take advantage of iCloud as well. As of this writing, the only apps that make use of iCloud are the ones created by Apple (see Figure 1-1), but expect iCloud to become more widely used as new versions of third-party apps are released.

Figure 1-1. iCloud can sync a lot of apps out of the box, and more are on the way!

Sharing Everywhere

You already know that you can share lots of things easily in Mountain Lion, but just mentioning that feature in passing doesn't do it justice. You share things by clicking the new button found in many Apple apps (see Figure 1-2).

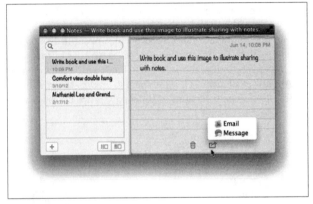

Figure 1-2. Sharing a note

Clicking that button invokes what Apple calls a Share Sheet— a menu of all the ways you can share the thing you're viewing. You could, for example, share a web page via Twitter, send someone's contact info via email, or post a tweet. Exactly *how* you can share the information depends on what app you're using. With Contacts, you can email, message, or AirDrop the card. With a web page, you get even more choices, as Figure 1-3 shows.

Twitter Abounds

One of the options on Share Sheets is Twitter. In fact, Twitter pops up in lots of the apps that come with Mountain Lion. That makes it super easy to quickly post stuff on Twitter, but half the fun of tweeting is the replies you get. So why would Apple include easy access to Twitter without giving you an easy way to hear about replies? It didn't: Mountain Lion's new Notification Center (described next) takes care of that half of the Twitter experience.

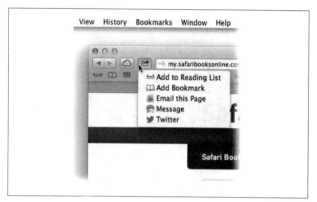

Figure 1-3. Options for sharing a web page

Notification Center

In earlier versions of OS X, notifications consisted of badged icons (like the little red spot showing how many messages you have in Mail) and notices that you couldn't miss, like when your Mac informed you that there were software updates available. But notifications have gotten much better in Mountain Lion. With the addition of Notification Center (Figure 1-4), you get to control exactly which apps (or even which people) can notify you and what kind of notifications you receive. That level of control wasn't available in earlier versions of OS X.

If you take a look at the desktop in Mountain Lion, you'll notice a Notification Center symbol in the upper-right corner (the icon is supposed to look like a bulleted list). Clicking this symbol displays your most recent notifications. And Mountain Lion doesn't just stick to the old-school notifications you're used to: you'll see notifications from all kinds of apps, including Game Center, Safari, Messages, Mail, FaceTime, and Calendar, among others. Even Twitter comes along for the ride, and Twitter isn't even an app!

Figure 1-4. A central repository for all your notifications

But you don't *have* to click that weird symbol to see your notifications: Notification Center can let you see them as they arrive, as shown in Figure 1-5.

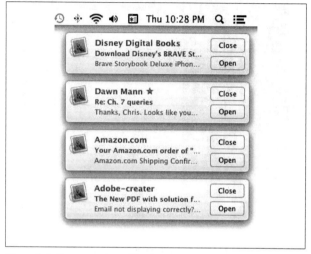

Figure 1-5. Banner-style notifications

If you're worried that the notifications may be too intrusive or annoying, relax. A trip to the Notifications preference pane lets you control how you're notified and which apps can notify you. See "Notifications" on page 134 to learn how to fine-tune notifications.

Reminders

One app whose notifications you'll probably want to keep turned on is Reminders (Figure 1-6). If you've used an iOS device, Reminders is already familiar; if you haven't, Reminders is simply an app that lets you set up a list of things to do. The list is then shared over iCloud so you can be reminded to go to that doctor's appointment or buy milk no matter whether you're sitting in front of your Mac or out running errands with your iPhone.

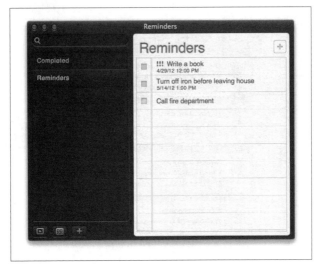

Figure 1-6. Reminders are finally on all your Apple devices

NOTE

If you like the location-based Reminders on your iPhone (like the "put on mask" reminder that pops up when you're outside the bank), you'll be happy to learn that you can use location-based reminders with Mountain Lion as well. See "Reminders" on page 197 for the details.

Notes

Notes is another app that started life in iOS and now shows up in Mountain Lion (Figure 1-7). Like the other apps brought over from iOS, Notes shares and syncs over iCloud: Write a note on your Mac, and it shows up on your iPad. You can create

---

notes that include text, videos, and photos. For more info, see "Notes" on page 194.

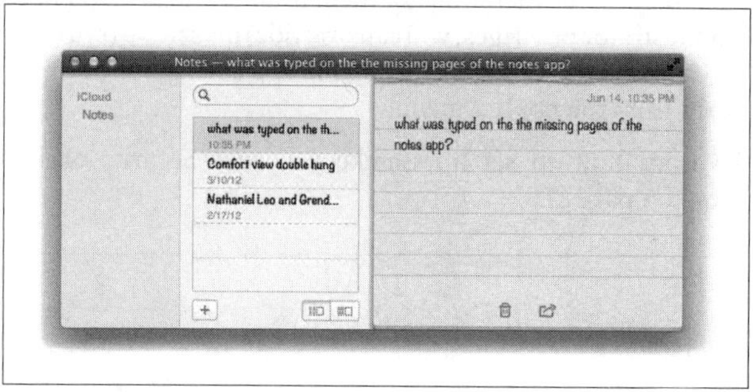

Figure 1-7. Notes is finally on your Mac

Updated Updating

If you've used previous versions of OS X, you're undoubtedly well acquainted with the Software Update item in the Apple menu. Selecting it used to bring up a maddeningly slow blue bar of progress while your computer checked to see what updates were available. Once that process finished, your Mac would either tell you everything was up to date or, more likely, that there was a new version of iTunes available, or was an update for iPhoto with enhanced support for RAW images for some obscure camera model.

Happily, those days are over. When you select the Software Update option in Mountain Lion, the App Store launches. The process is now faster, *and* you can see just which apps need updating without having to click Show Details (see Figure 1-8). Any software that you've purchased through the App Store will get updated, not just apps published by Apple.

Gatekeeper

Gatekeeper—which is part of the Security & Privacy preference pane (Figure 1-9)—is Apple's effort to minimize the chances of malware (malicious software) showing up on your Mac. Gatekeeper lets you decide, ahead of time, what apps you can install based on where you got them from (though, if you have administrator privileges, you can override this setting on a case-by-case basis by Control-clicking the app's icon and choosing Open from the pop-up menu.

To learn how to set up Gatekeeper, see "Security & Privacy" on page 128.

Figure 1-8. Updating apps

Messages

If you look for iChat in Mountain Lion, you won't find it; like the dodo, iChat is dead. But just because iChat is gone doesn't mean you have to stop chatting. The new Messages app retains all the functionality of iChat and adds much more. In Messages, you can send unlimited messages to anyone who uses an Apple device. And even better, because everything's instantly synced with iCloud, you can now go straight from

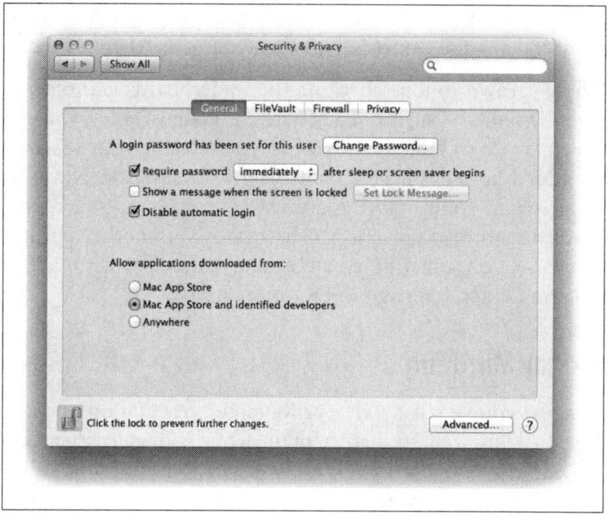

Figure 1-9. Setting up Gatekeeper

chatting using your Mac to chatting using your iPhone without a break in the conversation.

You can send texts from Messages, chat using your Jabber (or other popular chat program) account, start a FaceTime conversation with your buddy stationed at the South Pole, and so forth. It's like Apple has rolled all your communication needs into one convenient app.

Even better, like iMessage (the iOS app that inspired Messages), when you're contacting other Apple-gadget aficionados, you won't run up their cellphone bills: texts you send with Messages don't count against their cell providers' text-message limits. (Those message limits still apply for *non*-Apple cellphones and other devices, however.)

Game Center

According to Apple, the most popular portable gaming device in the world is the iPod Touch. If you spend a lot of time gaming on your iOS-based device, it stands to reason that you might want to keep the games going when you're using your Mac.

You've grown to love checking the leaderboards and playing online friends with your iPad. With the Game Center, you can now play those same friends when you're using your Mac. As an added bonus, since Game Center is included in Notifications, when you're playing against your cheating sister, say, you'll be notified as soon as she makes yet another cheater move so you can immediately take corrective action. See "Game Center" on page 184 for more info.

AirPlay Mirroring

Imagine you've got a video or Keynote presentation on your Mac that you want to share with the world—or at least a group of people too large to comfortably watch it on your Mac. With AirPlay Mirroring, you can stream what's on your screen to an Apple TV. Have a web page you want to show the entire class? Turn on AirPlay Mirroring, and all your students can see that page on the big screen. Miss your favorite show last night? If it's available online, you can broadcast it from your Mac to your big-screen TV.

Using AirPlay Mirroring is easy: just open the Displays preference pane (see "Displays" on page 137) and select Apple TV from the drop-down menu (or the menu extra that's enabled by default). The hardest thing about AirPlay Mirroring is parting with $99 for the required Apple TV.

Dictation

You've been able to talk to your Mac and have it perform actions for a decade. Now, Apple has raised the bar by giving your Mac the ability to take dictation system-wide. That means that anything you need to type you can instead *speak* to your attentively listening Mac, and the machine will type if for you.

NOTE

Dictation uses two things that might surprise you: your location and your contacts. Your location is understandable (regional accents and all), but contacts can seem positively creepy. Just what is Apple after? Turns out Apple doesn't care who your contacts are; it's interested in getting the names right when you use the dictation software.

Apple's version of dictation works a little differently than most people expect. After you press the Fn (function) key twice, a little microphone appears and you're ready to start dictating. But the words don't appear on the screen as you speak. Instead, once you're done dictating, you click the Done button and the stuff you just said is sent back to Apple's servers and deciphered, then the passage pops up on your Mac.

How well does it work? Here's the "transcript" of the first paragraph in this section:

> "you talk to your form actions for a decade now apples raise the bar in your Mac usually to take dictation system one that means anything you need to type you can Cenesti to your listening machine will type for"

Expect dictation to get better as time goes by.

But Wait, There's More!

That's 10 nifty new features in Mountain Lion, but this list isn't comprehensive. There are a bunch of smaller improvements throughout OS X in the various apps and system preferences; these changes are covered throughout this book. To learn about changes to a specific app, for example, flip to the section about that particular app.

CHAPTER 2

Installing Mountain Lion and Migrating Data

The easiest way to start enjoying OS X Mountain Lion is to buy a new Mac—the operating system is preinstalled, and you get a brand-new computer to boot! If you're one of the lucky ones getting a new Mac, you likely want to learn how to get all your important data from your old machine to the new one; see "Moving Data and Applications" on page 23 for details.

However, you don't *have* to buy a new Mac to run Mountain Lion, and since transferring your data is a little time consuming, you might not want to. If your Mac meets Mountain Lion's requirements (explained next), you can simply upgrade your old Mac to Apple's latest and greatest. This chapter gives you the lowdown.

What You Need to Run Mountain Lion

With every revision of OS X, Apple leaves some Macs behind, and Mountain Lion is no exception. To install Mountain Lion, your Mac has to possess a 64-bit Intel Core 2 Duo processor or better, be able to boot into the OS X 64-bit kernel, and have an advanced GPU (graphical processing unit). But those kinds of requirements are hard to commit to memory—ask 100 Mac users what GPU chipset their machine employs, and the vast majority of them will give you a puzzled look (the people who *do* know the answer are hard-core types and should be left alone).

So how do you find out whether your Mac is compatible with Mountain Lion? The simplest way is to try to buy the software from the App Store. If your Mac isn't compatible, the App Store will tell you that the software won't run on that machine.

If you want to download the software once and install on multiple machines, here's a list of Macs that can run OS X Mountain Lion:

- MacBook Pro 13-inch from mid-2009 or newer
- MacBook Pro 15-inch from late 2007 or newer
- MacBook Pro 17-inch from late 2007 or newer
- MacBook Air from late 2008 or newer
- Mac Mini from early 2009 or newer
- iMac from mid-2007 or newer
- Mac Pro from early 2008 or newer
- Xserve from early 2009 or newer

You also need 2 GB of RAM (which some otherwise compatible MacBooks and Mac Minis might not have) and 5 GB of disk space. These are, of course, *minimum* requirements; you'll be happier and your Mac will run more smoothly if your computer has more RAM and disk space than these requirements.

In addition to the hardware requirements, your Mac must be running OS X 10.6.7 (Snow Leopard) or later. Why not, say, 10.6.3? Well, it's likely that you'll be getting Mountain Lion from the Mac App Store, which didn't exist until 10.6.7 was released. If you're running Snow Leopard, just head to →Software Update to make sure you have the current version. If you're running Leopard, you'll need to find a copy of Snow Leopard and install *that* before you worry about anything else.

Preparing for the Install

Before deciding whether you actually want Mountain Lion, you should do a little detective work. Like OS X Lion, Mountain Lion doesn't support PowerPC apps, so if you depend on one of those for day-to-day work, you'll likely want to avoid Mountain Lion or upgrade to new apps before you install Mountain Lion. But how do you know which apps will and won't work?

Luckily, there's a quick way to get at this information. Head to ⌘→About This Mac, and then click More Info to display a two-column window. The left column contains a long list of entries that reveal specific information when you select them. Scroll down to the Software section, click Applications, and, in the right column, you'll see a list of all the apps you have installed. The list is sortable, so if you click Kind (as shown in Figure 2-1), the list will organize the applications into five categories: Intel, Universal, PowerPC, Classic, and (if your Mac just doesn't know what kind it is) blank. If the application you need says "PowerPC" or "Classic" next to it, then it won't run in Mountain Lion, so check to see if there's a new version available before you update your operating system. If you don't need any of those clunky PowerPC apps or if you're able to upgrade to newer versions of them, you're ready for Mountain Lion.

Installing Mountain Lion

If you've installed Lion, installing Mountain Lion will be familiar, as the process is almost exactly the same. If you're unfamiliar with the process, this section tells you what to expect.

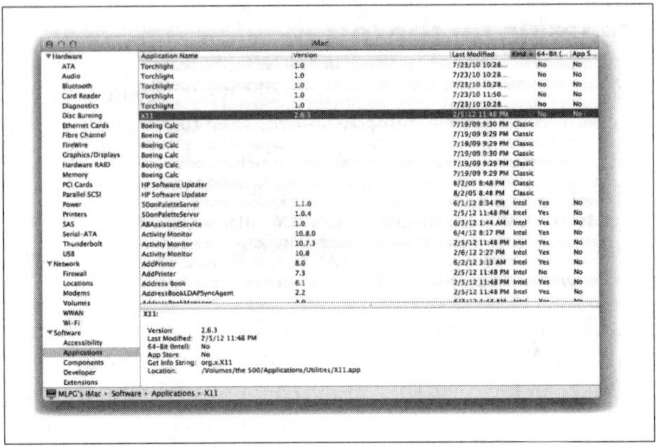

Figure 2-1. Know what will run before you upgrade

NOTE

This is the first edition of OS X that's App Store exclusive. With Lion, you had an option to pay for a thumb drive with the installer on it, but you can get Mountain Lion only from the App Store. So what if you have a slow Internet connection or bandwidth limits? Then you can visit your friendly neighborhood Apple Store and download Mountain Lion while you browse all the cool Apple hardware.

Regardless of whether you download the installer in the comfort of your own home or use someone else's bandwidth, the process of installing Mountain Lion is dead simple. First, make sure you're running the latest version of Lion or Snow Leopard (if not, head to →Software Update). Then, open the App Store (click its icon in your Dock), purchase Mountain Lion, and then wait for it to download.

NOTE

Be warned: the Mountain Lion installer is 4.35 GB. With a 5 MBps Internet connection (about the average speed in the U.S.), that will take roughly two hours to download. So if you have a pokey Internet connection or a bandwidth cap, you probably won't want to download a copy for each computer you have. In that case, you'll find the Mountain Lion installer in your Applications folder. Once you make a copy, you can transfer it to any other authorized Mac you want Mountain Lion on and run it without the hassle of a new download. (You'll still have to be connected to the Internet when you install Mountain Lion, but you won't have to download 4.35 GB of data again.)

Once the download is complete, the Mountain Lion installer should launch automatically. (If it doesn't, you'll likely find an alias for it in your Dock and the original application in your Applications folder.) All you have to do to get things moving is click the Continue button (Figure 2-2).

Figure 2-2. You have one option: Continue.

Once you take the plunge, you'll be presented with a page requiring you to agree to the software license. To install Mountain Lion, you'll have to click Agree twice: once in the Install OS X window and once on a drop-down menu that asks if you *really* meant that first click. After that, you'll see a message telling you where Mountain Lion will be installed. If you have multiple disks and don't like the choice the installer made, then click Show All Disks and you'll be able to pick the destination (Figure 2-3).

Figure 2-3. You get to choose the destination

Once you choose, click Install and then enter your administrator password to continue. Mountain Lion will show you a status bar indicating the progress of the install. A few minutes later, you'll be notified that you can either restart your Mac to proceed with the install or wait 30 seconds and let Mountain Lion restart for you. Instead of a regular restart, your machine will shut down, reboot, and then proceed with the installation process, which could take a while depending on how fast your Mac is.

NOTE

Mountain Lion can be installed on any drive (internal or external) that's formatted with Apple's Mac OS Extended (Journaled) file system. You can run Disk Utility from the installer's Utilities menu to format or inspect the drives on your system.

After the Install

After Mountain Lion is done installing, your Mac will restart *again* using the new operating system, and you'll be ready to use your new OS. You might see a message that says your email needs to be upgraded to work with the new version of Mail. Other than that, you can get back to using your Mac just like you did before you installed Mountain Lion (with some cool new features, of course).

If you installed Mountain Lion on a blank drive or a partition, your Mac will need some more information to get you up and running. You'll have to select your country's keyboard layout and time zone (Mountain Lion can do this for you; you'll see a checkbox labeled "Set time zone automatically using current location"). Then you'll be offered the opportunity to transfer data from another Mac (the next section explains the process). If you choose not to, click Continue. If you *do* want to migrate your data, see "Moving Data and Applications" on page 23 to learn how. Next, Mountain Lion will try to connect to the Internet. It'll automatically choose a network option, but if you're not happy with its choice, click the Different Network Setup button in the lower left of the window and choose your preferred network. Once you're hooked up to the network, you'll be asked for your Apple ID. You can skip this step, but if you have an iCloud account, using that as your Apple ID (by typing your ID and password into the provided box) will let your Mac use the associated services without your having to do any more configuring.

NOTE

You might be reluctant to sign up for yet *another* online account. You probably don't need another email account, and you might wonder about the utility of iCloud since you don't see a place for it in your computing life. Now is a good time to rethink that latter position. When Apple first released MobileMe (the precursor to iCloud) the service handled Mail, Contacts, and Safari bookmarks. In Mountain Lion, iCloud handles all the stuff MobileMe handled *and* syncs photos and documents, and lets you access your Mac remotely. In other words, iCloud is becoming so central to the OS X experience that continued resistance is futile.

After you enter (or create) your Apple ID, you'll be offered the opportunity to register your copy of Mountain Lion. The information you type into the registration form will be used not just to garner you a spot in Apple's database, but also to generate an address card for you in Address Book and to set up your email address for use with Mail.

Mountain Lion will then ask you for some info on how and where you intend to use your Mac. Once the data collection is out of the way, you'll be prompted to set up a user account. Mountain Lion will generate a full name and account name for you; if you don't want to use its suggestions, you can type in your own names. You'll also have to enter a password and, if you wish, a hint in case you forget the password.

With your account created, Mountain Lion will give you the chance to snap a picture for the account with a webcam, choose a stock image, or grab one from your picture library. Once that's done, Mountain Lion will configure your Mac using your iCloud information (if you use the service). If you're not an iCloud subscriber, don't worry—your Mac is ready to go. The things that iCloud configures automatically (like Mail) just won't be set up for you.

Moving Data and Applications

Not everyone will install Mountain Lion from the Mac App Store; some folks will have a new Mac with Mountain Lion preinstalled. If you're one of these lucky ones, you aren't interested in how to install Mountain Lion. But if you're upgrading from an older Mac or from a Windows-based PC (getting data from a Windows PC onto your Mac is a new, very nifty feature of Mountain Lion), you'll certainly be interested in getting that mountain of data from your old machine onto your new computer. Apple has an app for that: Migration Assistant, which can transfer files, settings, and preferences from your old computer to your new one. After running Migration Assistant, your new Mac will seem a lot like your old Mac. If you're transferring data from a PC, your new Mac won't seem like your old PC, but it *will* have the PC's data on it.

TIP

You might not want to migrate your data from an old computer right away: playing with a factory-fresh system is fun, and migrating data isn't a once-in-a-lifetime opportunity—you can do it whenever is convenient. So toy with your new Mac for a while, and *then* migrate your data using Migration Assistant.

When you run Migration Assistant, it can transfer the following things to your new machine if you're moving data from a Mac:

Users

All your user accounts will be moved to your new Mac. Accounts retain the same privileges (or restrictions) that they had before. If you try to move over a user that already exists on your Mac, you'll have the option to either change the account's name or replace the existing user (as long as you aren't logged in as that user; if you want to import settings into your account, first use System Preferences→Accounts to create a new user, log in as that user, and then run Migration Assistant again). See "User Accounts" on page 33 for more information.

Applications
All the applications in the Applications folder are transferred, so you won't have to reinstall them, and most should retain all their settings (including any registration or activation needed to run them).

Settings
Have a bunch of saved networks and passwords in your Network Preferences? They all come along for the ride. So, if you're used to automatically jumping on the local WiFi hotspot, you'll get on without any extra effort. If your screensaver requires a password to get back to the desktop, it still will. There are three suboptions under Settings: Time Zone, Machine (computer settings other than network or time zone), and Network; you get to pick and choose the ones you want to move to your new machine.

Other files and folders
If your Mac has files strewn everywhere, even if they aren't where OS X expects them to be (the Documents directory), they'll be transferred.

NOTE

If you stashed any files in the System folder, they *won't* get transferred. But you shouldn't ever stash anything in the System folder, as it can get modified at any time (by security updates and the like).

Migration Assistant *doesn't* move the following items:

The System folder
> You're installing a new system, so you don't need the old System folder to come along.

Apple applications and utilities
> Migration Assistant assumes that every Apple application (like FaceTime and iCal) on your Mountain Lion machine is newer or the same version as the corresponding item on the Mac you're transferring data from, so those applications won't get moved. Instead, Migration Assistant will keep the preferences the same and let you use the newer version. This is a problem only if you hate the latest version of iMovie (for example). If you want to use the older version instead, you'll have to manually move it over.

If you're transferring data from a PC, Migration Assistant will transfer the following:

- IMAP and POP accounts from Outlook and Outlook Express
- Contacts from Outlook, Outlook Express, and Contact home directory (a folder in Windows for your contacts)
- Calendars from Outlook
- Your iTunes library
- Home Directory content (Music, Pictures, Desktop, Documents, and Downloads)
- Localization settings, custom desktop pictures, and user settings

How you begin the process depends on what type of machine you're migrating from. If you're moving info from a PC, you'll need to point a browser to *http://support.apple.com/kb/DL1415*. From there, you can download a program to install on your PC that makes the process painless.

If you're using a Mac, Migration Assistant was installed when you installed Mountain Lion. As you'd expect, you need to be logged in as an administrative user (or be able to supply the username and password of an administrative user) to run Migration Assistant. Also, all other applications have to be closed. So save all your work and quit everything before you launch Migration Assistant. Then go to Applications→Utilities→Migration Assistant to get started.

If you haven't migrated data since the MacBook Air came out, the process has changed a little bit. In the days before the Air, Migration Assistant used FireWire Target Disk Mode (see the Note on page 28): you'd start the computer you wanted to transfer data from in this mode, plug it into the destination Mac, and then Migration Assistant took care of the rest. The good news is that this method still works if you have two computers with FireWire; the better news is that even if you don't have two Macs with FireWire, you can still use Migration Assistant. In fact, Migration Assistant offers two ways to get your old data on your new Mac (shown in Figure 2-4):

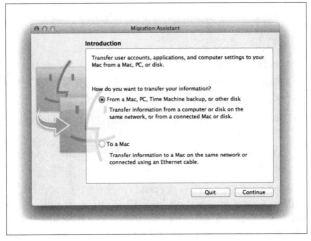

Figure 2-4. Starting the migration process

From another Mac, PC, Time Machine backup, or other disk
    Choosing this option allows you to transfer data from a Mac or PC that's either wired to or on the same network

(wired or wireless) as your new Mountain Lion-powered Mac.

To a Mac

This option is the counterpart of the "From another Mac or PC" option—you select this option on your source machine and the other one on your destination machine.

If you choose the first option, you'll get two *more* options to choose between:

From a Mac or PC

This is the option you'll use if you want to transfer data, well, from another Mac or PC. When you select this option and then click the Continue button, the next screen will warn you that all your applications must be closed. Save anything you've been working on and click Continue, and your Mac will start looking for other computers to transfer data from. Unless you've selected the "To another Mac" option (discussed above) on the computer you want to transfer data from, it won't find any. No problem: Migration Assistant will keep looking while you fire up Migration Assistant on the other machine and select "To another Mac" on that computer. Once both computers are ready to go, you'll see something like Figure 2-5.

Click Continue and you'll see a passcode. You don't have to write it down or remember it; you just need to make sure it's the same as the one displayed on the machine you are transferring data from. (The passcode won't show up on the data-donating machine until the exchange has been initiated by the Mac you're moving the data *to*.) Verify that the numbers match, and then click Continue. Next, you get a chance to decide what you want to migrate (see "Fine-Tuning Data Migration" on page 30). Click Continue, and your data will be transferred.

From a Time Machine backup or other disk

If you choose this option, your new Mac will scan all attached drives and then present you with a list of drives you can migrate data from. Click the one you wish to use, and

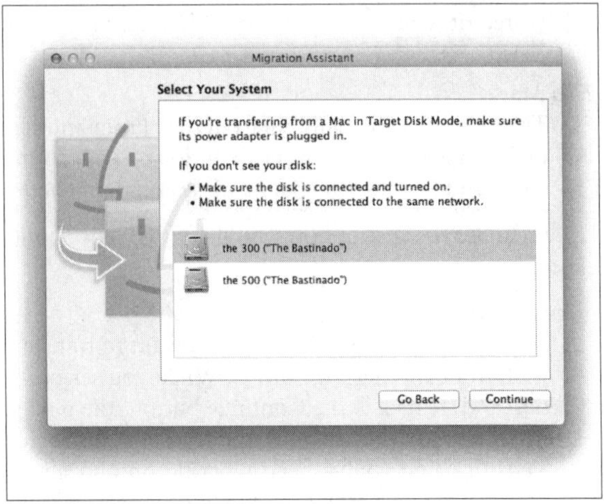

Figure 2-5. Transferring data from a disk

then click Continue. By default, Mountain Lion will transfer all your relevant info, but you can change that behavior (see "Fine-Tuning Data Migration" on page 30).

NOTE

If both Macs have FireWire, choose "From a Time Machine backup or other disk" and then restart the Mac you want to get data *from* in FireWire Target Disk Mode. You do this by holding down the T key while the computer boots until you see a FireWire symbol dancing on the screen.

Networking Options When Migrating Data

Before Migration Assistant came along, getting your data onto your new Mac could be a real pain. While Migration Assistant is a fantastic tool, it has one drawback: it doesn't differentiate between different types of networks.

As you know, not every network connection is equal. If you're transferring small bits of information (like email or text messages), a cellphone protocol is plenty of bandwidth. But when you're transferring larger chunks of data, the connection type is more important. If you're using Migration Assistant, there's a good chance that you're planning to send a bunch of data from your old computer to your new Mac, so the speed of the transfer really matters—especially since you'll be locked out of both machines for the duration of the transfer.

Here are your data-transfer options from fastest to slowest:

Thunderbolt

> You couldn't use Thunderbolt when Lion was released, not because some Macs didn't have the port for it, but because there wasn't a cable available from Apple. Now you can get the required cable from Apple for $49. It's an investment you might want to make if you have a lot of data to transfer, because Thunderbolt can transfer data at up to 20 gigabits per second.

Ethernet

> Ethernet is your second-fastest option. If your Mac has an Ethernet port (all Macs except the MacBook Air do), you can string an Ethernet cable between your old computer and your new Mac and transfer data at up to a gigabit per second.

FireWire 800

> FireWire 800 is your next-fastest option. Not every Mac that can run Mountain Lion has a FireWire 800 port, so if you're unsure, check your System Information (see "System Information" on page 213) and select FireWire. If both your computers are FireWire 800 equipped, you'll be swapping data at a peppy 800 Mbps. A lot of Mac owners have FireWire *400* on their old machines and FireWire *800* on their new ones (no new Macs have FireWire 400). If you're in that camp, you can get a FireWire 400 to 800 cable (try Amazon) and then transfer your files using a 400 Mbps connection.

WiFi

WiFi is the slowest option. Its speed varies depending on the network, but if you're using the 802.11n, your network could be running up to 300 MBps.

The speeds listed above are best-case scenarios, so your real-life experience may not match those numbers. But even with that caveat, you'll save a significant amount of time if you use one of the wired options instead of WiFi.

NOTE

Your Mac is kind of lazy. It doesn't care which transfer method is the fastest; it'll automatically opt for the network connection you're currently using. So if you don't want to sling files over your WiFi connection (which could take forever), you can string a Thunderbolt cable between your Macs and then switch to *that* connection in the Network preference pane to get your data moving at breakneck speed.

Fine-Tuning Data Migration

If you're migrating data, chances are you have a new Mac. If you're like most people, you've accumulated a lot of cruft over time, and you might not want to transfer *everything* from your old Mac. Of course you'll want to save that folder of lolcat pictures, but that folder with your master's thesis is just taking up space.

Migration Assistant lets you decide what to take and what to leave behind in terms of users and settings. (Don't worry: this is a nondestructive process, so the data you shun on your new Mac will still be on the old machine.) Simply follow the data-migration process described earlier in this chapter, but when you get to the "Select Items to Migrate" screen (Figure 2-6), uncheck the items you want to leave behind. Click the disclosure triangle to display all your options.

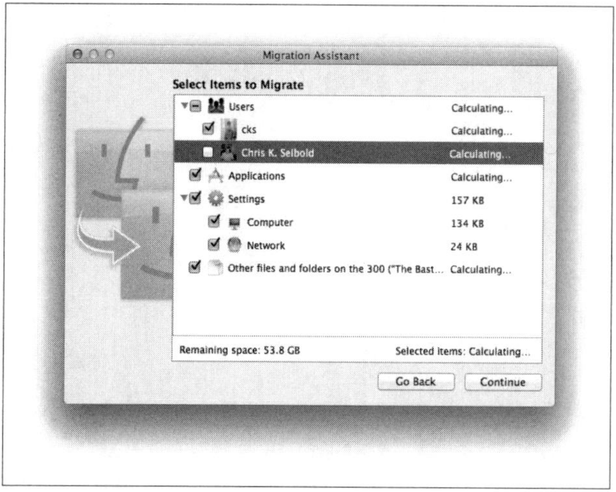

Figure 2-6. Choosing what data to grab

NOTE

Don't get confused by the folder names listed on the "Select Items to Migrate" screen. For example, Movies doesn't mean that Migration Assistant will import all your movie files, just that it will import the Movies *folder*. If you have movies stored elsewhere and you want them to come along during the transfer, make sure the "All other files and folders" option is checked.

After you make your selections, click Continue and your data will be transferred. Give it some time and the data will magically appear on your new Mac.

Once Migration Assistant finishes transferring your data, Setup Assistant will pop up and offer to upgrade your email (if you're migrating from an older version of Mac OS X). This takes a few moments, but once it's finished, you're free to use your new Mac and pick up where you left off with your old machine!

CHAPTER 3

A Quick Guide to Mountain Lion

What You Need to Know About OS X

Finding your way around Mountain Lion for the first time is exciting, but it's also easy to miss many of the cool new features, especially if you're new to OS X or you've been using an older version of it. This chapter will get you up to speed on the basics of OS X, with a special focus on what's new in Mountain Lion. It'll familiarize you with the key aspects of OS X so you can get the most out of Apple's best operating system to date.

User Accounts

The logical place to start is with the first thing you created when you installed or ran OS X for the first time: your account. Mountain Lion's roots go all the way to Unix, a multiuser workstation and server operating system. Because OS X is based on Unix, it's also multiuser to its core. Even if no one but you ever touches your Mac, it's still helpful to understand user accounts, because you may need to deal with them someday.

Consider these situations:

- As you'll learn shortly, you may want to set up an unprivileged account for day-to-day use to limit your vulnerability to mistakes and malicious software.

- If you ever need to run a demonstration on your Mac, you'll probably want to create a separate account to run the demo to prevent interruptions from chat buddies, calendar reminders, and the like.

- Even the most solitary Mac user eventually needs to let someone else use her Mac (a houseguest, a family member, or a TSA agent), and it's so easy to set up a new user account that you may as well do it. Then even your most reckless friend can use your Mac without much threat of major chaos.

There are six types of user accounts in OS X, and you can also create groups of users:

Administrator

When you create your first account in OS X, it'll automatically be an Administrator account. This is the most powerful type, because an administrator can make *global* changes that affect the computer and all other user accounts, like adding and removing programs. Because of this ability to change things (sometimes inadvertently), most savvy Mac users argue that you shouldn't use Administrator accounts for day-to-day computing; instead, they recommend using a Standard account most of the time.

NOTE

You might detest the idea of jettisoning the power of the Administrator account for day-to-day use. But even if you're using a Standard account, you can still make global changes by typing in your Administrator account name and password.

Standard

Standard accounts are the sweet spot: you can't mess up your Mac or anyone else's account while using a Standard account, but you still have plenty of control over how your Mac works. You can add and delete programs for just your account, but not to the entire system, and you can delete files you own (meaning ones you've created or installed), but not files owned by others.

Managed with Parental Controls

Accounts managed with Parental Controls are limited in what they can do. These users can't make changes to the system at all. If you tried to use a managed account, you'd likely find it frustrating and unacceptable; but to a five-year-old, a managed account is nirvana. You can adjust the settings using the Parental Controls preference pane (see "Parental Controls" on page 158).

Sharing Only

Sharing Only accounts are designed to let people connect to your machine from another computer to share files. People assigned this type of account can't log into your Mac via the login screen; only remote connections are accepted.

Group

You can use Group accounts to create a collection of multiple users. These types of accounts let you exercise fine-grained control over privileges for shared documents.

Guest

If you want to let others use your Mac without the ability to accidently delete precious files or install malicious software, you can enable the Guest User. This creates an option on the login screen to log in as, unsurprisingly, Guest. There's no password required, and you're free to lock the account down using Parental Controls. Guests can use your Mac as they wish while they're logged in, but the moment they log out, everything they've done (documents they created, emails they've sent, etc.) gets deleted.

(Note that the Guest Account *isn't* an option if you have FileVault activated; see "FileVault tab" on page 131.)

Setting up accounts

Now that you know the different types of accounts in Mountain Lion, you'll likely want to set up a few. Click →System Preferences→Users & Groups (located in the System section). Before you can make any changes, you have to click the lock icon at the bottom left of the preference pane and then enter an administrator username and password. The extra level of security is there because this preference pane lets you adjust the level of access for other accounts, so you wouldn't want an unauthorized person making changes.

To add a new account, click the + button above the lock icon. This opens a drop-down window where you can select the type of account to create, enter the identifying info (full name, account name), and set up a password. Mountain Lion assigns a default image as the new user's picture. To pick a different image, just click the default image in the middle of the preference pane. You'll be able to choose from the icons included with Mountain Lion or snap a pic with your Mac's built-in iSight camera and then apply Photo Booth's effects to the image (click the "Apply an effect" button in the snapshot's lower right). Setting up an account is significantly more fun in Mountain Lion than in previous versions of OS X.

To enable the Guest account, click Guest User in the list of accounts, and then check the box marked "Allow guests to log in to this computer." To disable this account, simply uncheck that same box; this will prevent guests from using your computer without a password.

The Home Folder

The Home folder is what makes your Mac seem like *your* Mac. For example, if you create a document and save it in Documents, the document doesn't show up in some centralized documents folder for the entire system; it shows up in only the Documents folder that lives inside your Home folder.

This pattern extends to other folders, too (Music, Movies, Pictures, and so on). Each account you create gets its own Home folder with a subset of folders inside it. This is where all your files and personal preferences (like your selected desktop background) are stored. All the home folders are stored in a folder called Users that's found in the top level of your drive.

NOTE

There's one folder inside the Users folder that doesn't correspond to any user: the Shared folder. You can use it to store files and folders you need to share among users on the same Mac.

You can access your Home folder by opening a Finder window and then either clicking the house icon in the sidebar or choosing Go→Home (Shift-⌘-H). In every Home folder, you'll find the following subfolders:

Desktop

This is where all the files sitting on your desktop are stored. (There are a few other types of items that can appear on the desktop—hard disks, CDs, DVDs, iPods, and servers—but you won't see them in this folder.) If you drag a document from this folder to the Trash, it'll disappear from your desktop.

Documents

This is where your Mac saves documents by default. Using this folder isn't mandatory, but it does offer a level of convenience to have a central repository for all your documents. You can add subfolders for even more organization: just open the Documents folder and then choose File→New Folder (Shift-⌘-N).

Downloads

The Downloads folder serves double duty: it lives in your Home folder and has a spot in your Dock. Anything you download from the Web via a browser shows up here (unless you change the default download location in your browser's preferences, that is) *and* in your Dock in the Downloads stack (the stack bounces when a new item finishes downloading). If you click the Save button next to an attachment in Mail, it's also saved here. You can get your downloaded items either by opening this folder or by going to the Downloads stack in the Dock.

Movies

This folder is much like the Documents folder, only it stores all the movies you make with iMovie and screencasts you make with QuickTime Player. Just as with the Documents folder, there's no reason to store your movies here other than convenience.

Music

The Music folder, not surprisingly, is where you can store music files. It's also where iTunes stores its music library and any iTunes purchases you make, including iPhone/iPod apps and videos.

Pictures

Toss all your *.jpg*, *.png*, and *.gif* files right in here. iPhoto also uses this folder to store images you add to iPhoto.

Public

The Public folder is a repository for files you want to share with other users who can log into your Mac. You can get to another user's Public folder by switching to the Finder and choosing Go→Computer. You'll see a window showing all the drives and networks coupled to the Mac you're using. Selecting the startup drive will reveal a folder called Users. Open that folder, and you'll see all the other users' Home folders (they're labeled with the respective users' names, as shown in Figure 3-1). Open the appropriate person's folder, and you'll see her Public folder. You can grab any files stored in another user's Public folder and use them as you wish. Likewise, any files you toss into your Public folder can be grabbed by anyone using the same Mac. (Note that, while you can copy and modify any files you find in the Public folder, you can't actually change the contents of someone else's Public folder.) If you want to share files in this folder with people on *other* computers, you'll have to go to the Sharing preference pane (see "Sharing" on page 155).

Figure 3-1. This Mac has a meager number of accounts, but even if you have 100 accounts, they'll all be stored in the Users folder

To receive files from others who use the same Mac, have them put the files in your Drop Box, a folder inside your Public folder. Drop Box is a shared folder, but the sharing goes only one way: people can put things into your Drop Box, but they can't take anything out. In fact, they can't even see what's in this folder. To use Drop Box, enable File Sharing (see "Sharing" on page 155).

Sites

You'll see this folder only if you're using an Administrator account. If you want your Mac to host a website (it's certainly capable), then this is where you put the files for the site. You'll need to do more than add an HTML file to this folder to get your site working, though. See "Sharing" on page 155 to start sharing sites stored in this folder over your local network.

Where's My Library Folder?

Before Mac OS X Lion, there was one additional folder inside the Home folder: Library. This is where your preferences and settings (among other things) are stored. If you're used to manually controlling various aspects of your Library folder, you'll likely miss having easy access to it.

It turns out the Library folder isn't really gone; it's just invisible. The easiest way to make it appear is to head to the Finder and click the Go menu. With that menu open, press the Option key, and the Library folder will magically appear as a menu item. Click it and you can get back to manually messing about with your Library folder if you're so inclined (but be warned that tweaking items in the Library folder can have unintended consequences).

Using Mountain Lion

Once you have Mountain Lion running and your system set up, what do you need to know to use it? This section teaches you the basics of starting up your Mac, getting around after it's booted, and shutting the machine down.

Starting Up

Chapter 2 covered what happens when you turn on a fresh, out-of-the-box Mac (or a new install of Mountain Lion). Each time you boot up your Mac after that, the startup experience is usually seamless. As you'd expect, your Mac will boot into Mountain Lion (unless you tell it otherwise).

NOTE

If you've installed Boot Camp (see "Boot Camp Assistant" on page 210) or another operating system, you can set the default startup disk with the Startup Disk preference pane (see "Startup Disk" on page 169).

The first thing you'll see when you start your Mac is the gray Apple logo, followed by the spinning wheel that resembles a circle of perpetually falling dominoes. Once your Mac finishes booting, you'll be presented with a list of users or a username/password prompt, depending on your settings (see "Logging In" on page 42 for more details); log in and you'll be transported to OS X.

Thanks to Resume, all the apps that were running when you last turned off your Mac can automatically open with all the windows you had before. But, unlike Lion, you'll have to tell OS X to use Resume. To get Resume resuming, when you shut down or log out of your Mac, a dialog box that appears includes a "Reopen windows when logging back in" checkbox. Check that box and, when your Mac finishes starting up, all your windows will be just how you left them!

Startup key commands

Before you start booting up your Mac, you can press and hold one of the following keys/key combinations/buttons to change how it starts (useful when troubleshooting).

Key command	Action
Mouse button	Ejects any media in the optical drive.
C	Forces your Mac to start up from a CD or DVD in the optical drive.
R	On Macs with built-in displays (MacBooks and iMacs), resets the display back to the factory settings.
T	If the Mac has a FireWire or Thunderbolt port, boots the Mac in Target Disk Mode; to get out of this mode, restart the machine. You don't have to specify which port you're using; your Mac will figure it out for you.
⌘-S	Boots in Single User Mode, which starts your Mac with a text-only console where you can perform some expert-level system maintenance.
⌘-V	Boots in Verbose mode, which shows all the kernel and startup messages while your Mac is booting.
Shift	Boots in Safe Mode, a reduced-functionality mode that forces your Mac to check its startup disk, load only the most important kernel extensions, disable fonts not in the /System/Library/Fonts folder, and more.
Option	Invokes Startup Manager and allows you to select which OS to boot into; useful if you have multiple copies of OS X installed or use Boot Camp to run other operating systems.

Logging In

When you start up your Mac after creating an account, you'll be greeted by the pic you snapped or the image you chose when you set up the account and a place to type your password (don't forget it!). This is different from previous versions of OS X, which automatically logged you in (no typing that pesky password) when your Mac was booted. If you want the old behavior back, you can enable it by visiting the Users & Groups preference pane and manually enabling Automatic Login. Simply click the lock icon in the panel's lower left, click Login Options, and then use the "Automatic login" menu to select the user who's automatically logged in.

WARNING

Automatic Login makes using your Mac more convenient, but it's also a security risk, since anyone who starts
your Mac has all the privileges you've granted yourself.
So enable this feature only after careful consideration.

The Login Options settings are also where you can control fast
user switching (which is on by default). This feature lets you
switch users without having to log off, so the applications that
you have running keep going while another user logs into her
account. However, having more than one user logged in can
use up quite a bit of memory, so if your computer is already
kind of slow, you might want to turn this feature off.

If you leave fast user switching on, look for an icon or username
on the right side of the menu bar. Click this name or icon and
then use the drop-down menu to select another user to log in
as someone else. If you turn fast user switching off, you'll have
to log out (→Log Out) before you can log in as a different
user.

Logging Out, Sleeping, and Shutting Down

Using the Mac is great, but at some point you'll want to *stop*
using it. When you reach that point, you've got a few options:

Shut Down

> To shut down your Mac, click   →Shut Down. Click Shut
> Down in the dialog box that appears (or do nothing for
> one minute), and your Mac will power off. It should take
> only a few seconds to do so. The next time you want to
> use your Mac, hit the power button and wait for the ma-
> chine to boot.

Log Out

> To close your current work session and quit all running
> programs but leave your Mac running, click   →Log Out
> or press Shift-⌘-Q; then click Log Out in the dialog box
> that appears. (Pressing Shift-*Option*-⌘-Q instead logs you

out immediately—there's no confirmation dialog box.) To use your Mac again, you (or another user) will need to log in.

Sleep

You don't have to shut your Mac down every day; you can just let it sleep. To put a MacBook to sleep, all you have to do is close the lid. On desktop Macs, select →Sleep or press Option-⌘-⏏ (these methods work on MacBooks, too). A sleeping Mac uses very little electricity, and it'll wake up in seconds. (For more on saving energy, see "Energy Saver" on page 138.) Wondering if your Mac is sleeping or simply off? On MacBooks, you'll see an indicator light that pulses to let you know it's only sleeping.

Shut down and log out shortcuts

No one wants to spend lots of time logging out or shutting down. Here are some keyboard shortcuts that make those processes faster.

Key command	Action
Shift-⌘-Q	Logs you out
Shift-Option-⌘-Q	Logs you out without a confirmation dialog box
Control-Option-⌘-⏏	Shuts your Mac down immediately (with no confirmation dialog box)
Control-⌘-⏏	Restarts your Mac with no confirmation dialog box
Control-⏏	Displays a window that lets you restart, put to sleep, or shut down your Mac
Control-⌘-power button	Forces your Mac to shut down (use this only as a last resort)
Option-⌘-⏏	Puts your Mac to sleep

Mountain Lion Basics

A lot happens between when you start up your Mac and when you shut it down. The time you spend in OS X will be more pleasant and productive if you learn where everything is. The logical place to start the tour is at the top of your screen.

The Menu Bar

The menu bar spans the top of your monitor (if you use multiple monitors, you can choose which one the menu bar shows up on using the Displays preference pane). The left side of the bar provides access to commonly used commands, and the right side is reserved for menu extras (see "Menu extras" on page 53), Spotlight (the magnifying glass icon), and (brand-new to Mountain Lion) the Notification Center (the banners icon). Every Mac user's menu bar is likely to look a little different, depending on what's installed and how the Mac is configured. A typical menu bar is shown in Figure 3-2.

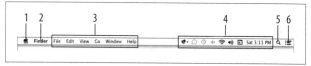

Figure 3-2. A typical menu bar

NOTE

If you haven't used Lion, then Mountain Lion's Full Screen feature will be new to you. Full Screen applications use your entire screen—even the pixels used by the menu bar—to let you get the most out of the app. The menu bar isn't gone when you're using full screen apps, it's only hiding. To get the menu bar back, just move your cursor to the top of the screen, and the bar will reappear.

Here's what you'll find in the menu bar, from left to right:

1. The Apple menu ()
2. The Application menu
3. A set of application-related menus
4. Menu extras
5. Spotlight
6. Notification Center

NOTE

Hate the translucency of the menu bar? You can turn the bar solid gray by selecting →System Preferences→Desktop & Screen Saver→Desktop, and then unchecking the "Translucent menu bar" box.

The Apple menu

No matter which application you're using, the options in the menu are always the same (Figure 3-3).

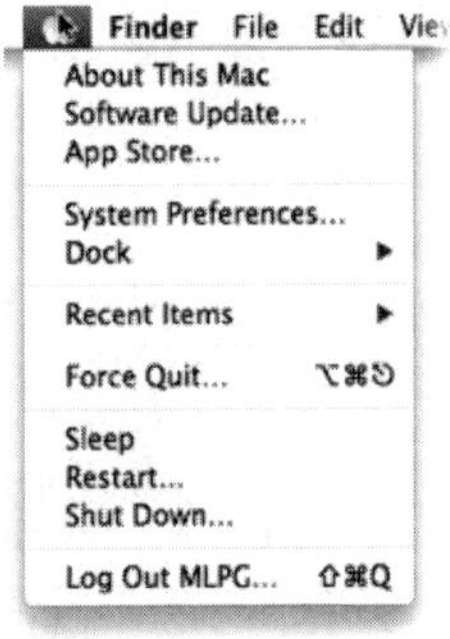

Figure 3-3. Mountain Lion's Apple menu

Here's what each menu item does:

About This Mac

Pops up a window giving you a quick overview of your machine: the version of OS X it's running, the processor it has, and the amount of RAM that's installed. There are three things you can click in this window:

- Click the version number (such as 10.8) to cycle through the build number of OS X and the serial number of your Mac. (It's not unusual to need this info when getting support over the phone.)

- Click Software Update to launch the App Store and see what updates are waiting for you.

- Click More Info to open the System Information window, which has a tab that gives you an overview of your Mac, and ones that tell you (in a cool graphic fashion) about Displays, Storage (drives attached to your Mac), and Memory (how much you have installed and in which slot). You'll also find tabs for Support (a good starting point when you're problem solving) and Service, which lets you check your warranty status and gives you a chance to buy AppleCare (Apple's extended warranty service).

Software Update

Software Update has been upgraded in Mountain Lion. When you click Software Update, you won't see a blue bar crawling across your screen like in previous versions of OS X. Instead, the App Store launches, and you'll be notified of any updates for Apple software and apps you've purchased from the App Store.

NOTE

It's easy to get too reliant on the Software Update
feature, but it's important to remember that running Software Update doesn't help with software
that you didn't purchase via the App Store. So, for
example, if you're using a copy of Word 2011 that
you downloaded from Microsoft's website, you'll
have to go to its site to check for updates instead.

App Store

Launches the Mac App Store, where you can look for new
applications, check for updates to ones you already have,
and so on.

System Preferences

Launches System Preferences, which is covered in detail
in Chapter 5.

Dock

Opens a menu that lets you quickly configure your Dock:
Turn Hiding On, Turn Magnification On, and three Dock
positioning options (you can put it anywhere but the top
of your screen). The Dock Preferences option, not surprisingly, opens the Dock preference pane. For more info,
see "Dock" on page 124.

Recent Items

Displays a menu showing your 10 most recently used applications, documents, and servers. You can change the
number of items displayed here by going to System Pref-
erences→General, and then adjusting the "Recent items"
setting.

Force Quit

Forces stubborn applications to quit. For more on this
command, see the section "Misbehaving Applications" on page 104.

Sleep

Puts your Mac into sleep mode, a low-power mode that
preserves what you were doing before you put your

machine to sleep. When you wake it up, everything will be just as you left it. To wake a sleeping Mac, just press a key or move the mouse. You can set your Mac to automatically sleep after a period of inactivity by using the Energy Saver preference pane; see "Energy Saver" on page 138.

Restart

Makes your Mac shut down and then immediately reboot and go through the entire startup process. You'll be asked to confirm that you really want to restart your Mac. Unless you click Cancel, your Mac will restart one minute after you select this menu option.

Shut Down

Powers your Mac down. It'll stay shut down until you press the power button, unless you've set a time for your Mac to auto-start in the Energy Saver preference pane (see "Energy Saver" on page 138).

Log Out

Logs you out of your user account. The next person who uses your Mac will have to log in.

NOTE

Many items in the menu have ellipses (...) after them. These indicate that a confirmation dialog box will appear if you select that option. If you want to restart, shut down, or log out *without* seeing the dialog box, hold the Option key while selecting the action of your choice from the menu.

The Application menu

Next to the menu is the Application menu. The name and contents of this menu depend on what application you're currently using. Figure 3-4 shows the Finder's Application menu, which you see whenever you have a Finder window or click an empty spot on your desktop.

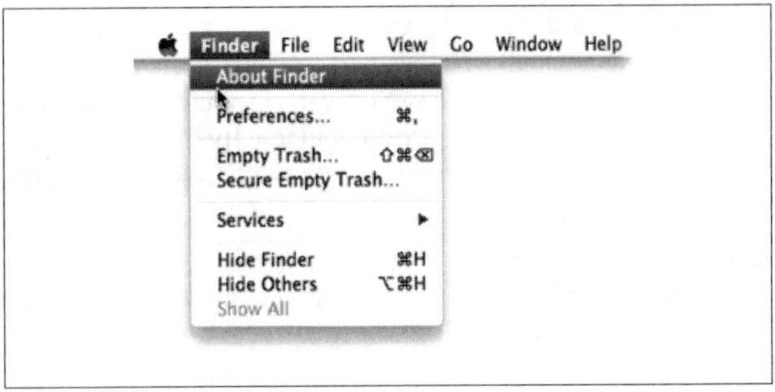

Figure 3-4. The Finder's Application menu

There really isn't a standard Application menu, but most have some commonalities. In a typical Application menu, you'll find:

About [Application Name]
> Opens a window with the application's version number, copyright info, and whatever else the program's developer thinks should be there.

Preferences
> Opens the application's preferences window. What you can control from this window varies from application to application—it could be very little or a lot. For info on the Finder's preferences, see the section "Mastering the Finder" on page 57.

Services
> All the services that the current app can use appear in a list when you highlight this option. Check out "The Services Menu" on page 51 for details.

Hide [Application Name]
> Hides all of the current application's windows. If you have 50 Safari windows open and don't want to manually minimize each one to see what lies beneath, then choose this option. To get the windows back, just click the application's Dock icon.

Hide Others

Hides every application except the one you're using.

Show All

This is the antidote to the Hide command. Whether you've hidden a single application or every application, Show All will return all the hidden application windows to full visibility.

Quit [Application Name]

Quits the current application. (You can also invoke this command by pressing ⌘-Q.) Most people's inclination is to quit any application they aren't using, but that often isn't necessary. OS X is very good at allocating resources, so leaving an application idling will generally have very little impact on the system.

The Services Menu

The Services menu is the most complex option in the Application menu. It offers you quick access to functions provided by other programs, which are called *services*. The services available to you depend on the applications installed on your Mac and the program you're using. In some applications, the Services menu won't have anything to offer (the menu will read "No Services Apply").

TextEdit (which you can find in the Applications folder) provides a nice example of what the Services menu can do. Figure 3-5 shows the options available when you've selected some text in TextEdit. If you want to send the selected text as a Mail message, for example, all you need to do is choose New Email With Selection, and Mail will pop open a new message with the text already inserted. Clicking the Services Preferences option opens the Keyboard preference pane to its Services section, where you can customize the Services menu. You can also create your own services with Automator (see "Automator" on page 174).

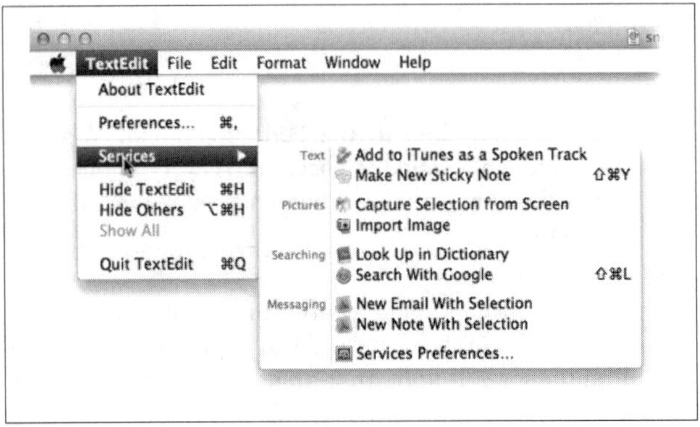

Figure 3-5. Services for TextEdit

Standard Application menus

After the Application menu come more menus. How many? That depends on the application. For example, Mail has eight and Safari has seven. You'll find at least four menus in the menu bar besides the Application menu. What's in these four menus *also* depends on the application, but there are some standard options to expect:

File

> This menu typically contains options for saving, opening, creating, and printing files. For apps that use iCloud, when you select Save in this menu, you'll get a choice to save the document locally or to iCloud.

Edit

> Here you'll find the old Mac standbys: Cut (⌘-X), Copy (⌘-C), Paste (⌘-V), and Undo (⌘-Z).

Window

> This menu lists all the open windows for the current application, as well as some commands for working with them.

Help

> Depending on the application and its developer, this menu can either be very useful or a waste of space. When

you open the Help menu (either by clicking it or by pressing Shift-⌘-?), you'll see a search box and a few other options. One of the really nice things about the Help menu in OS X is that it won't just regurgitate an entry in a database—instead, if possible, it *shows* you how to do what you want to do. For example, suppose you want to create a new folder while using the Finder. Open the Finder's Help menu, type **new folder** in the search box, and then put your cursor over the New Folder entry in the list that appears. The Help system will then show you which menu contains the New Folder option and highlight it with a floating blue arrow, as shown in Figure 3-6.

Figure 3-6. Help pointing out an answer

Menu extras

The right side of the menu bar is where you'll find the menu extras, a.k.a. menulets. (Spotlight and the Notification Center are on the bar's *far* right and aren't technically menu extras; you'll learn about them in a moment.) Menu extras give you easy access to functions you use often. The menu extra's icon usually reflects what it does. A useful example is the Keychain menu extra (Figure 3-7), which you can add by launching the Keychain Access utility in */Applications/Utilities* and then choosing "Show keychain status in menu bar" from its preferences. The lock icon that appears in your menu bar gives you quick access to your passwords and secure notes without having to make a trip to the Utilities folder.

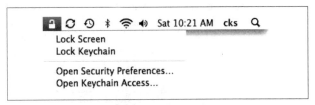

Figure 3-7. The Keychain menu extra

Not every menu extra is a shortcut to a program; some control settings (such as the Volume menu extra), and some are there to show the status of certain aspects of your Mac (such as the Battery menu extra). What menu extras you find useful depends on how you use your Mac.

Unlike menus, whose options change depending on the application you're using, menu extras remain constant: each one always does the same thing, no matter which program is running.

The menu extras you see by default depend on how your Mac is configured. You can banish unwanted menu extras by ⌘-dragging them off the menu bar; they'll disappear with a satisfying poof sound and an accompanying animation. To rearrange your menu extras, ⌘-drag them into any order you want.

The Accounts menu

If you've left fast user switching enabled (see "Users and Groups" on page 157), you'll see the name or icon of the current user here. Click it to select another user to log in as.

Spotlight

Clicking this magnifying glass icon brings up the Spotlight search box. For more information, see "Searching with Spotlight" on page 94.

Notification Center

The Notification Center is new to Mountain Lion, and it's a big improvement. Click its icon at the right end of the menu bar to reveal all your current notifications. To customize which apps can use Notification Center and how the notifications are displayed, see "Notifications" on page 134. If you want to open Notification Center quickly and your Mac has a trackpad, you can open it by placing two fingers on the far right side of your trackpad and then dragging them to the right.

Use the menu bar less

If you really want to be productive, it's much quicker to use keyboard shortcuts for most commands than to go hunting for them in the menu bar. Here's a list of some of the most commonly used keyboard shortcuts for items in the menu bar.

Key command	Action
⌘-C	Copies selected information to the Clipboard
⌘-V	Pastes the contents of the Clipboard into the current document
⌘-X	Cuts the current selection and copies it to the Clipboard
⌘-A	Selects everything (the entire document, all items in a folder, etc.)
⌘-S	Saves the current file (you can't use this one too often)
⌘-O	Opens a new file
⌘-W	Closes the current window
⌘-Z	Undoes your most recent action (some programs offer multiple levels of undo)
⌘-H	Hides the current application and its windows
⌘-,	Opens the current application's Preferences window
⌘-Q	Quits the current program (not available in Finder)

There are many more key commands at your disposal (see Chapter 8), but these are the ones you'll likely use most often. Also, each application has its own keyboard shortcuts that can streamline your workflow, so learning the key commands for the programs you use frequently is worth your time.

The Desktop

As you probably know, the big area under the menu bar is called the desktop. Open application windows float over the desktop and, depending on how you have it configured, the desktop will also show you all the attached and internal drives (iPods, flash drives, and so on), any optical disks (CDs, DVDs), and any files you've stored here for easy access. You can change your desktop's background either by Control-clicking or right-clicking the desktop and then choosing Change Desktop Background, or by heading to the Desktop & Screen Saver preference pane (see "Desktop & Screen Saver" on page 122).

To control how items are displayed on the desktop, choose Show View Options from the Finder's View menu, or press ⌘-J. The Desktop window shown in Figure 3-8 appears, which lets you control the size of desktop icons (from 16×16 pixels all the way to 128×128 pixels), how they're spaced (by tweaking the invisible grid that OS X uses when arranging desktop icons), and the size and location of their labels.

If you check the "Show item info" box, you'll see extra information when looking at items on your desktop. Drives show the name of the drive and the amount of free space left, folders list the name of the folder and the number of items contained in them, and DVDs show the amount of data stored on them. The extra information displayed for files depends on their type; image files, for example, display their size in pixels. The "Show icon preview" checkbox lets you toggle between generic icons and icons that display the file's contents. The "Sort by" menu lets you choose how desktop icons are arranged. You can have them snap to the (invisible) grid or be arranged according to some criteria (name, date created, and so on).

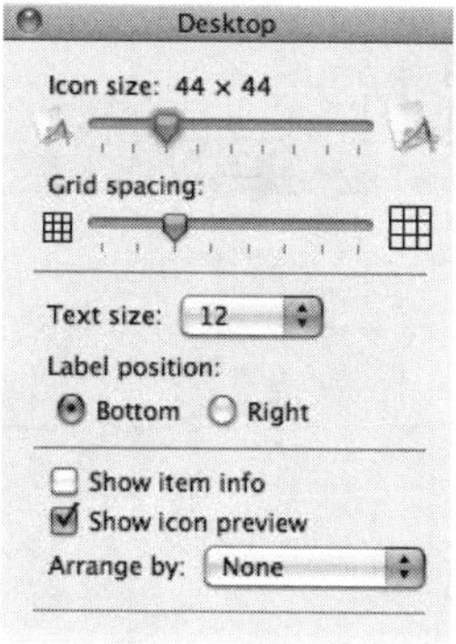

Figure 3-8. Customize how things appear on your desktop

To navigate around the desktop without using the mouse, you can use the arrow keys. Another option is to start typing an item's name; the item will automatically get highlighted, and you can open it by pressing ⌘-O; press the Return key instead to rename the item.

To control what kind of items appear on the desktop, you use the Finder's preferences (switch to the Finder and then choose Finder→Preferences or hit ⌘-,). Under the General tab, you'll find options to display (or hide) hard disks; external disks; CDs, DVDs, and iPods; and connected servers.

Mastering the Finder

Understanding the Finder is key to successfully getting around in OS X. It lets you move files, copy files, and launch applications, among other things. The most common way users interact with the Finder is through a Finder window.

To bring the Finder to the front, click some empty space on the desktop, click the Finder's Dock icon, or hit ⌘-Tab until you select its icon. Once the Finder is frontmost, hit ⌘-N to open a Finder window. Figure 3-9 shows a typical one.

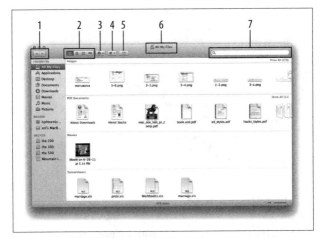

Figure 3-9. A standard Finder window

NOTE

Your Finder window might not look exactly like the one in Figure 3-9. If, for example, you've upgraded from an older version of OS X, you'll likely have a Quick View button not shown in Figure 3-9. Don't worry—the Finder's toolbar is highly customizable, as explained in the next section.

The Finder window includes several components:

1. Back and Forward buttons

These buttons cycle through directories you've been using. For example, say you start in your Home directory and then drill down into your Documents folder. After you find the document you were looking for, clicking the Back button returns you to your Home directory.

2. View controls

These buttons control how the Finder displays information. You have four options: Icon View (the default), List

View, Column View, and Cover Flow View; see "Finder views" on page 64.

3. *Action menu*

Clicking this button reveals a drop-down menu that varies depending on the item that's selected. Generally, it contains the same options you'd get if you right-clicked or Control-clicked that item.

4. *Arrange menu*

This button lets you change the order in which the items in a folder are displayed. It gives you nine different sorting options (plus the option to not sort at all).

5. *Share Sheet*

Clicking this button allows you to send the selected file via email, Messages, Twitter, or Flickr.

6. *Proxy icon and title*

This item is a graphical representation of your current location (for example, the drawer icon in Figure 3-9 shows that you're in All My Files). Right-click or Control-click it to bring up a list of common destinations; select one to hop to that spot or drag a folder onto the list to create a copy of it in that location.

7. *Search box*

Enter text in this box and hit Return to tell the Finder to search for matching items. New in Mountain Lion, when you start typing a search term, it displays a drop-down menu with suggestions to help refine your search. The search is powered by Spotlight, but unlike a Spotlight search, it won't include Mail messages or web pages in your results.

Customizing the Finder toolbar

To remove items from the Finder's toolbar, simply ⌘-drag them off the toolbar. Doing this tidies things up, but it doesn't give you what most people want: *more* options. To add things to the toolbar, either right-click or Control-click a blank space in the toolbar and then select Customize Toolbar, or go to

View→Customize Toolbar. Either way, the dialog box in Figure 3-10 opens, showing all the items you can add.

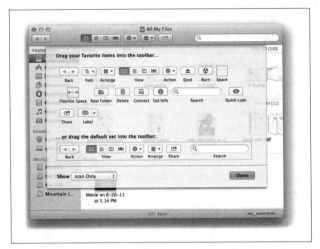

Figure 3-10. You can customize the Finder's toolbar to match your workflow

---

NOTE

The Show menu at the bottom of Figure 3-10 lets you change *how* items in the Finder's toolbar are displayed. You get three options: Icon and Text, Icon Only (the default), and Text Only.

Most of the items you can add are self-explanatory, but a few are worthy of a closer look:

Path

This button gives you a menu that shows the path up from the current directory to the top level of your computer. For example, suppose you have the Finder open to your Pictures folder. Clicking this button will reveal the following list:

- Pictures
- [Your Home folder]
- Users
- [Your Boot Drive]
- [Your Computer]

You can choose any item in the list to jump to that directory.

Burn

Burn a lot of disks? This button can save you a lot of time. Select an item (or folder) and then click this button, and the Finder will tell you to insert a disk to burn to.

Get Info

This brings up the Info window for the selected item— very useful if you adjust permissions often.

The sidebar

The sidebar occupies the left-hand side of a Finder window and is reminiscent of iTunes's sidebar; it's divided into three sections:

Favorites

This section lists the most common things you'll use: All My Files, AirDrop, Applications, Desktop, Documents, Downloads, Movies, Music, and Pictures. Some of these items point to actual folders (like Applications, for example), but not all of them do. All My Files points to all the files you've created; it's a Smart folder (see "Smart Folders" on page 87) that contains files you're most likely to be interested in.

NOTE

AirDrop, which made its debut in Lion, provides a zero-configuration way of sharing files with other users nearby. When you click the AirDrop icon, your computer starts looking for nearby Macs. When it finds one, just drag the file you want to send onto the icon for that user in the AirDrop window. The recipient will get a notice that you want to transfer the file, and once he grants the request, the file will speedily move to his Mac. It's a slick system that doesn't rely on your WiFi network connection (AirDrop uses the WiFi built into your Mac instead), so you can share files with someone nearby even when you're not connected to a network. Not all Macs that can run Mountain Lion can use AirDrop (it depends on the WiFi chipset in your machine) so if you don't see the AirDrop icon in your sidebar, don't panic—your Mac just can't use the feature.

Shared

This section lists any shared devices available to your Mac. Computers shared via Bonjour, shared drives, Time Capsule, Back to My Mac, and the like show up here.

Devices

This is where you find the devices connected to your Mac, including internal drives, external drives, USB sticks, iPods, CDs, and DVDs.

NOTE

If your sidebar looks nothing like the one described here, don't panic. The sidebar can look different depending on how your Mac was set up previously, what you have plugged into your Mac, and other factors.

The sidebar is more than just a speedy way to hop to these locations. Want to install an application you just downloaded? Instead of opening a Finder window to the Applications folder, just drag the application to the Applications folder in the sidebar. To reorder items in the sidebar, simply drag them around; to remove items, just drag them off the sidebar. (Dragging an item out of the sidebar doesn't delete the item, it only deletes the reference to it from the sidebar.) You can do even more by right-clicking or Control-clicking an entry in the sidebar—a menu will pop up allowing you to do some common and useful tasks tailored to the item you clicked. Finally, if you want quick access to a folder, application, or document, you can drag it onto the sidebar and an alias will be created pointing to the item.

Finder preferences

Like every application, the Finder has a set of preferences you can customize. To access them, go to Finder→Preferences, or type ⌘-, while the Finder is the active application. The window that appears has four tabs:

General

> Here's where you determine what items show up on your desktop. Your options are hard disks; external disks; CDs, DVDs, and iPods; and connected servers. You can also specify what directory a new Finder window opens to. The default is All My Files, but you can change that to any folder by choosing it from the "New Finder windows show" menu. You also get a checkbox (that's unchecked by default) where you can choose to open folders in a new window. Finally, you can fine-tune (or turn off) spring-loaded folders, which automatically pop open if you drag an item over them, allowing you to quickly access nested folders.

Labels

> If you're big on organization, you can label folders with colors. By default, the labels' names match their colors— for example, if you label something with the color red, the

text label is Red. That isn't very descriptive, so if you want to have the red label read "En Fuego" instead, this is where you can change the label's name. (Note that changing a label's name won't affect how labeled folders are displayed.) To add a label to a folder, right-click or Control-click the folder and then choose the label you want to use from the menu that pops up.

Sidebar

This tab lets you specify which items are displayed in the sidebar. If you've deleted a built-in item from the sidebar, a trip to this tab can restore it. If you uncheck all the items in a category, that category will no longer appear in the sidebar. (If you've added any items to a section of the sidebar, that category won't vanish until you also remove those items by dragging them out of the sidebar.)

Advanced

The Advanced tab gives you checkboxes to control whether filename extensions are displayed (if you check this box, Safari will be displayed as Safari.app, for example), whether the Finder should warn you before changing an extension, whether you should be warned before emptying the Trash, and whether the Trash should be emptied securely (see "Trash" on page 80 for more info).

Finder views

You can change how items are displayed in the Finder by clicking the toolbar buttons (see Figure 3-9) or using the keyboard shortcuts listed below. Here are your options:

Icon View (⌘-1)

This is the default view. Items are displayed as file icons, application icons, or folder icons (Figure 3-11). Single-clicking an item in Icon View selects it; double-clicking launches the application, opens the file (inside its associated application), or opens the folder. You can use the arrow keys to move from item to item. Holding the Shift key while using the arrow keys selects multiple items.

Figure 3-11. Icon View of the Applications folder

List View (⌘-2)

This view presents the contents of a folder as a list. You can open subfolders by clicking their disclosure triangles (see Figure 3-12). List View offers more information than Icon View but feels more cluttered. As with Icon View, you can navigate through List View using the arrow keys: ↑ and ↓ change what's selected; → and ← open and close (respectively) a subfolder's disclosure triangle. To open all subfolders under the one that's selected, press Option-→; to close all subfolders after you've opened them, use Option-←. To sort files, click a row heading; the triangle in the heading indicates the sort order.

Column View (⌘-3)

Column View (Figure 3-13) is the favorite of a lot of users. While it looks a little like List View, it doesn't include any disclosure triangles. Clicking a folder in this view reveals the contents of that folder. If you continue all the way to a file, the last column will show a Quick Look preview of the file and some key information about it. For example,

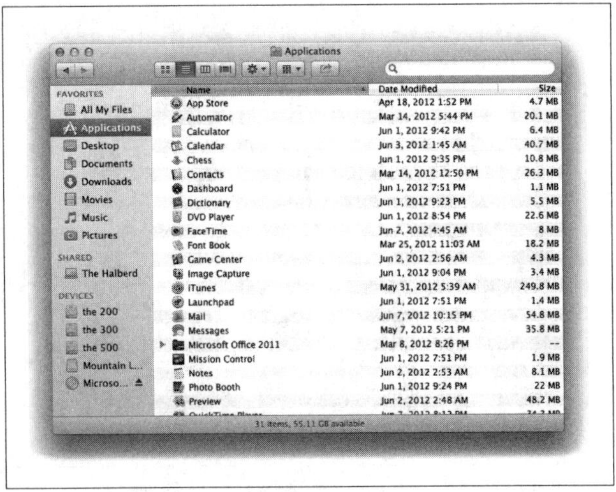

Figure 3-12. The useful List View

if you drill down to a movie, the film's preview will appear in the last column, and you can even play it right there. If you select an application, the last column will display a huge version of the program's icon and information about the application.

In Column View, the arrow keys work exactly as you'd expect, moving the selection either up, down, left, or right. Holding Shift while pressing ↑ or ↓ allows you to select multiple items in the same directory. To change the width of the columns, drag the two tiny vertical lines at the bottom of the dividers between columns; hold Option as you drag to resize all the columns at once.

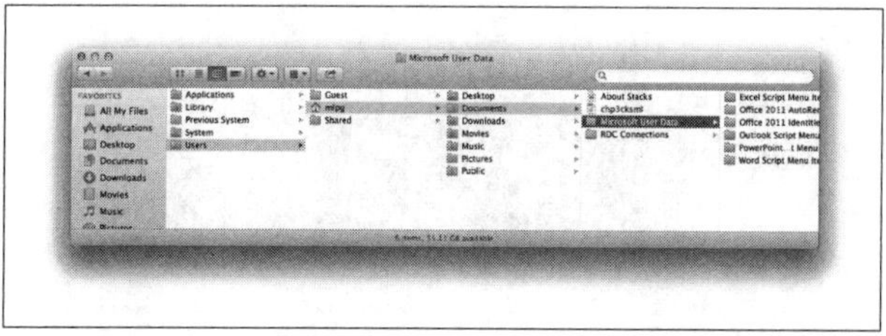

Figure 3-13. Column View is particularly useful for drilling down through stacks of folders

Cover Flow View (⌘-4)

Cover Flow View is very slick. If you use iTunes, an iPod Touch, or an iPhone, you're familiar with this view, shown in Figure 3-14. It displays the items in a directory as large icons. You can adjust the size of the Cover Flow area by dragging the three tiny horizontal bars below the previews; Mountain Lion will resize the icons accordingly.

In this view, the ↑ and ← keys move the selection up in the list below the Cover Flow area, whereas the → and ↓ keys move your selection down the list.

Figure 3-14. Cover Flow View—the go-to option if you want eye candy

Common Finder tasks

You'll end up using the Finder for many basic tasks. Want to rename a folder? Copy or move files? The Finder is your best friend. Here are some tasks you'll likely use the Finder for:

Rename a file, folder, or drive

In the Finder, simply click the icon of whatever you want to rename and then press Return. Mountain Lion highlights the name so you can type a new one. Hit Return again to make the new name stick.

Create a folder

To create a new folder, you can either choose File→New Folder from the Finder's menu bar, or press Shift-⌘-N. The new folder appears as a subfolder of whatever folder is currently selected. New folders are creatively named "untitled folder."

Quickly look inside a file

You can get a pop-up preview of a file's contents by using Quick Look. In the Finder, select a file, and then press the space bar or ⌘-Y, or click the eye icon in your Finder toolbar (if you don't see this icon in the Finder's toolbar, see "Customizing the Finder toolbar" on page 59 to learn how to add it). An easy-on-the-eyes window (like the one in Figure 3-15) pops up, displaying the contents of the file.

Quick Look is file savvy; look at a Word document and you'll see what's written on the page, look at a spreadsheet and you'll see rows and columns, look at a movie and it will start playing. All this without having to open the program associated with that file.

While Quick Look is visible, click a different file and Quick Look displays that file instead. Switch Finder windows (you can have a gazillion Finder windows open at a time) and Quick Look displays the item in the current window. You can even preview more than one file at a time with Quick Look: simply select multiple files, and arrows will appear at the top of the Quick Look window that you can use to flip through previews of all the files you selected.

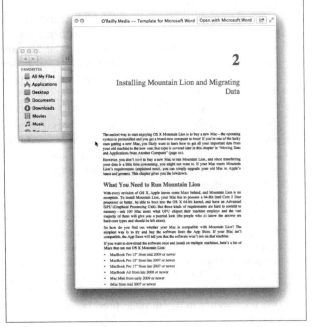

Figure 3-15. Dawn Mann edited this entire book using only Quick Look and Messages

Make an alias

There are times you want access to a file or folder without having to burrow through directories to get at it. Some people's first inclination is to move the item to a more accessible location, but the best solution is to make an alias. An alias acts just like the regular file or folder, but it points to the original: put something in a folder alias and it ends up in the original (target) folder. Delete the alias and the item it refers to is unaffected.

You can spot an alias by a curved arrow in the lower-left corner of its icon. To create an alias, select a file in the Finder and then choose File→Make Alias (or press ⌘-L). Then simply drag the alias to where you want it.

Duplicate files and folders

If you want a copy of a file or folder, click the item in the Finder and then select File→Duplicate (or press ⌘-D), and Mountain Lion generates a brand-new copy of that item with the word "copy" appended to its name. Your original item remains untouched while you hack away at the copy.

Copy files to a new location on the same disk

When you drag files from one spot to another on the same disk, OS X moves those files to the new location without making a copy. To *copy* files to another location on the same disk instead, hold Option while you drag the files to the new location. Once you release the mouse button, the original file(s) stay put, and you get a copy in the destination location.

Conversely, when you drag files from one disk to another, OS X *copies* them. To make it move them instead, hold down the ⌘ key while you drag.

Eject a drive or disk

If you've got external drives hooked to your Mac, at some point you'll want to eject them. Just yanking a drive out is a bad idea; if data is still being written to the drive, you might lose it.

You have a few ways of ejecting drives and disks. The classic way is to drag it to the Trash (when you do, the Trash's icon changes to an Eject icon). If you've got a Finder window open, you can also eject it directly from the sidebar—simply click the ⏏ next to the drive's icon. If a drive won't eject, Mountain Lion will tell you which application is using files on that drive (and preventing you from ejecting it).

If you want to remount a drive (use the drive after you've ejected it) that you left plugged in, you can either remount it with Disk Utility (*/Applications/Utilities/Disk Utility*) or simply disconnect the drive from your Mac and then reconnect it.

Reformat a disk

If you've got a new disk, it might not be in the right format. Most flash drives and many pocket drives come formatted as FAT32 disks, but some arrive unformatted. Your Mac prefers the Mac OS Extended (Journaled) file system, and if you don't need to share files with another operating system (such as Windows), this format is your best choice. To erase the drive and format it as Mac OS Extended (Journaled), head to */Applications/Utilities/Disk Utility*. Select the disk you want to reformat from the list on the left side of Disk Utility, click the Erase tab, select the format you want, and then click Erase. Remember: reformatting erases all the information on the disk.

Compress files and folders

If you're going to burn a bunch of data to a disk or if you want to minimize upload times, you can compress files and folders. Mountain Lion gives you an easy way to pull this off: right-click or Control-click a file, and then select Compress from the pop-up menu, and Mountain Lion creates a copy of that item with the same name, but with the suffix *.zip* appended. The amount of space this saves depends on the type of file: compressing a QuickTime movie (*.mov*) doesn't save as much space as compressing a folder full of text files does, for example.

Duplicating Optical Disks

DVDs and CDs are getting less popular for sharing files because of the availability of cheap flash drives, but they're still common enough that you might need to make backup copies of important data stored on a CD or DVD. If you have a desktop Mac, you could install two DVD drives and copy DVDs and CDs disk to disk, but that option is available only on high-end Macs (although you could use an external USB drive with other Macs). No worries, though; with Disk Utility, you can easily duplicate that DVD or CD and burn it to a different disk.

Fire up Disk Utility (*/Applications/Utilities/Disk Utility*) and then select the CD or DVD you want to copy from the list of available disks. Next, click the New Image button at the top of the window, choose "DVD/CD master" from the Image Format pop-up menu, and then choose a location with sufficient disk space from the Where pop-up menu. Click Save and Mountain Lion makes an image (a special type of copy) of the DVD.

Once the copying operation is complete, you'll have a perfect copy of the DVD or CD on your drive. To burn that copy onto a blank CD or DVD, select the disk image from the list on the left side of Disk Utility (if it's not there, drag the disk image from the Finder into the list), and then click the Burn button and insert a blank disk when prompted. (Alas, this approach won't work for copy-protected software or movies.)

The Dock

The Dock is a key aspect of OS X. It contains shortcuts to frequently used applications, folders, and documents, and shows you which applications are running by placing a blue dot under each one. (A lot of people detest the blue dots; fortunately, you can turn them off: just head to →System Preferences→Dock and then uncheck the box next to "Show indicator lights for open applications.") Figure 3-16 shows a typical Dock.

Figure 3-16. A typical Dock

You can use the Dock to switch among active applications; just click the Dock icon of the one you want to switch to, and that becomes the frontmost application. When an application is starting up, its Dock icon bounces so you can tell that it's loading. If an already-running application's icon begins bouncing, that's the Dock's way of telling you the application wants your attention.

The Finder is on the far left side of the Dock and is always running. To the right of that, you'll see application icons, a dotted-line divider, the Applications stack, the Downloads folder, any minimized windows, and the Trash.

NOTE

If you upgraded from an older version of OS X, you'll likely see a Documents stack in your Dock as well. You may also find that what appears as a stack and what appears as a folder differ from what's listed here. Don't be alarmed: these differences won't affect the way your files are stored.

Since the Dock is conveniently located, it's a natural way of opening your most-used applications and documents. The obvious question is how do you add items to the Dock? The process is simple: just locate the application or document you want to add and then drag it onto the Dock. Keep in mind, though, that you can put applications only on the left side of the Dock's divider and you can put documents only on the right side of the divider. (Even if you haven't placed an application or a document in the Dock, it will appear there as long as it's running or open.) Adding items to the Dock doesn't move or change the original item, and removing items from the Dock doesn't delete them from your Mac.

To arrange items in the Dock, simply drag them into the order you want. (Dragging a running application that's not already in the Dock permanently will add it.)

TIP

If you want to open a particular document in a specific application, drag the file onto that application's icon in the Finder or Dock, and that application will generally try to open the file. However, some applications respond differently: dragging something onto the Mail icon, for example, attaches it to a new message.

Once your Dock is fully loaded with applications and documents, it can get a little overwhelming. If you forget what that minimized window is for or what application will start if you click a certain icon, the Dock can help you out. Simply put your cursor over the Dock item in question and a text bubble pops up with info about that item, as shown in Figure 3-17.

Figure 3-17. Oh, so that icon represents the App Store...

Removing items from the Dock is easy: drag the unwanted item off of the Dock or onto the Trash icon, or right-click or Control-click the item in question and, in the pop-up menu that appears, select "Remove from Dock." (Remember, this removes the item only from the Dock—the file remains on your Mac.

NOTE

There are two things about the Dock that you can't
change: the Finder is always on the left end of the Dock,
and the Trash is always on the right end. You can't move
them, and you can't put anything on the far sides of
them. Think of the Finder and the Trash as two book-
ends that expand to accommodate all the items in between.

Dock Exposé

Ever wanted to see all the windows an app currently has open?
You can accomplish that easily with Dock Exposé. The way
you pull this off is really slick: pick any running application,
click and hold its icon in the Dock, and then select Show All
Windows in the pop-up menu that appears. You then see
something like Figure 3-18. Any minimized windows show up
as small versions below a subtle dividing line. Click any window to bring it to the front.

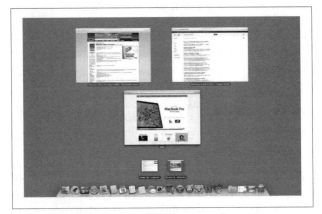

*Figure 3-18. Safari's open and minimized windows displayed using
Dock Exposé*

The pop-up menu that appears when you click and hold an application's Dock icon also lets you quit or hide the selected application. The menu also includes an Options submenu to let you keep the application in the Dock, set it to open each time you log into your computer, or show it in the Finder.

Dock menus

Every item in the Dock has a Dock menu. To access this menu, right-click or Control-click the item's icon. What shows up in the menu depends on what you click and, in the case of an application, whether it's running and what it's doing. Application Dock menus typically include relevant commands. For example, if you're currently playing a song, iTunes's Dock menu lets you mute your computer, skip and rate songs, and so forth. All applications' Dock menus include these options:

- Options→Keep in Dock or Remove from Dock, depending on current setting
- Options→Open at Login (saves you a trip to the Users & Groups preference pane)
- Options→Show in Finder (reveals where the application resides on your Mac)
- Hide (hides all the application's windows; equivalent to pressing ⌘-H)
- Quit (closes the application; you'll be warned if there are any unsaved changes; equivalent to ⌘-Q)

The Dock menus for stacks (such as the Documents or Downloads stack) offer a different set of choices:

- Sort by options (Name, Date Added, Date Modified, Date Created, Kind)
- Display as (Folder or Stack)
- View content as (Fan, Grid, List, Automatic)
- Options ("Remove from Dock" or "Show in Finder")
- Open [stack name]

Stack view options

That folder or jumble of icons (depending on how your preferences are set—jumbled icons is the default) on the right side
of your Dock is called a *stack*. You can choose which view to
use for each stack by opening its Dock menu (the previous
section explains how). Here are your options:

Fan View

This is the default view for stacks. If you click a stack that's
set to this view, it'll fan out, making it easy to choose the
item you're looking for, as shown in Figure 3-19. Fan View
is nice when there aren't a lot of items in a stack; it's less
helpful when there are more than a dozen or so items. If
you use the arrow keys to select items in the stack, a blue
highlight appears behind the current item; hit Return to
open it.

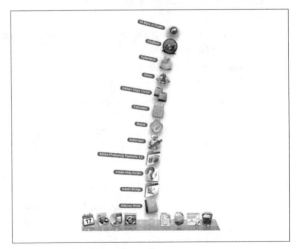

Figure 3-19. Fan View of a stack

Grid View

In Grid View (Figure 3-20), you get to browse by icon, and
you can use the arrow keys to highlight an item. If that

item is an application or a document, hitting the Return key starts the application or opens the document. If the selected item is a folder, hitting Return opens *another* Grid View window that displays the folder's contents.

Figure 3-20. The useful Grid View

List View

List View (Figure 3-21) displays the stack's items as a list on the same background used by Grid View. List View is a bit pedestrian compared list Fan View or Grid View, but that doesn't mean it's useless. You can scroll through the list using the ↑ and ↓ keys, and when you run across a folder, pressing the → key opens a submenu of the enclosed items.

Automatic View

If you don't feel like fine-tuning the way a stack is displayed, you can let Mountain Lion pick a view for you based on the stack's contents. Simply right-click or Control-click the stack and then choose Automatic from the "View content as" section of the pop-up menu.

Figure 3-21. List View of the Downloads folder

Trash

It doesn't matter whether you've got a relatively tiny SSD drive in a MacBook Air or 4 terabytes of hard disk space in a fully tricked-out Mac Pro. Sooner or later, you're going to want to get rid of some files, either because your drive(s) are feeling cramped or you just don't want the data around anymore. That's where the Trash comes in.

The Trash is located on the right end of the Dock (or, if you've moved the Dock to the left or right of your screen, it's on the bottom; see "Dock" on page 124 to learn how to relocate the Dock). To banish files from your Mac, select them and then drag them from the Finder to the Trash (or press ⌘-Delete).

When the Trash has something in it (whether it's one item or a million), its icon changes from an empty mesh trash can to one stuffed with paper. This lets you know that the files you've moved to the Trash are still there, and that you can retrieve them (until you empty the Trash).

To open the Trash and view its contents in a Finder window, click its Dock icon. (You can view the items in the Trash with the Finder, but you can't actually open a file that's in the Trash; attempting to do so will result in an error message.) If you find something in the Trash that shouldn't be there, you can either drag it out of the Trash or select it and then click File→Put Back to send it back to where it was originally.

To *permanently* delete items in the Trash, right-click or Control-click the Trash's Dock icon and choose Empty Trash, or open the Finder and either choose Finder→Empty Trash or press Shift-⌘-Delete.

Note that emptying the Trash doesn't completely remove all traces of the files you deleted. Those files can be recovered with third-party drive-recovery utilities, at least until the disk space they previously occupied has been written over with new data. To make it harder for people to recover deleted data, in the Finder, choose Finder→Secure Empty Trash. This command overwrites the deleted files multiple times.

If you work with a lot of sensitive files, you can tell the Trash to *always* write over files you delete by going to the Finder's preferences (Finder→Preferences or ⌘-, while in the Finder) and, on the Advanced tab, checking the box next to "Empty Trash securely." You probably want to leave the "Show warning before emptying the Trash" option checked because, once you securely empty the Trash, you're not getting that data back.

Dock preferences

Here are a few quick and easy changes you can make without invoking the Dock's preference pane. If you right-click or Control-click the divider between the two parts of the Dock (it's a subtle, dark-gray line), you'll get the pop-up menu shown in Figure 3-22. This menu lets you choose whether to automatically hide the Dock when you're not using it, change the magnification of icons in the Dock, change the Dock's location, change the animation OS X uses when you minimize windows, and open the Dock's preferences.

You can change the size of the Dock by dragging up or down over the dashed divider to increase or decrease the Dock's size, respectively.

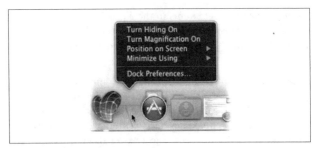

Figure 3-22. A quick way to make Dock adjustments

The Application Switcher

The Dock is the most obvious way to switch among applications while they're running, and Mission Control is probably the niftiest way, but Mountain Lion gives you a third way to flip among open apps. The aptly named Application Switcher (Figure 3-23) lets you switch applications without taking your hands off the keyboard, a huge timesaver if you change programs often. To use it, just hit ⌘-Tab.

Figure 3-23. Change apps and keep your fingers on the keyboard

Holding the ⌘ key while repeatedly hitting the Tab key cycles through the open applications from left to right, and then wraps around to the first application on the left again (use Shift-Tab instead to go the opposite direction). Alternatively, you can press ⌘-Tab and then, while still holding down ⌘, use the ← and → keys to move between applications. When the application you want to switch to has a white border around it, release the keys and that program will come to the front.

Standard Window Controls

Most windows in OS X share some characteristics, shown in Figure 3-24. Knowing what they do will help you be much more productive when using Mountain Lion.

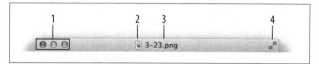

Figure 3-24. Mountain Lion's standard window controls, which live on the title bar

Here's what these controls do:

1. The red button closes the window; if you point your cursor at it, you'll see an × or—if there are unsaved changes to the current document—a dark-red dot inside it. The yellow button minimizes a window; put your cursor over this dot, and you see a –. The green button maximizes the window and displays a + when you point to it.

2. This is called the proxy icon. Drag it to create an alias of the current file, or Option-drag it to copy the current file.

3. The name of the current file.

4. If the application you're using can go full screen, you'll see these arrows. See the section "Full-Screen Applications" on page 84 for details.

The following table lists some keyboard shortcuts that are useful for working with windows.

Action	Key command
Open a new window	⌘-N
Close the active window	⌘-W
Minimize the active window	⌘-M
Minimize all windows for the frontmost application	Option-⌘-M

NOTE

Not every key combination is universal. For example, some applications use ⌘-M for something other than minimizing the active window.

Resizing Windows

If the green maximize button isn't convenient for you, you can manually resize windows in Mountain Lion. To pull this trick off, put your cursor over the edge of a window and, when the cursor changes to a double-headed arrow, simply drag to resize the window.

NOTE

You'll still see the occasional triple-slash resizing handle in the lower-right corner of programs such as Microsoft Word. Don't worry, you can still resize such program windows by dragging any edge, though the resize handle works, too.

Full-Screen Applications

Ever longed for a more immersive Web-browsing experience, or wished that iCal would take over every pixel of screen space? Having Safari fill your screen when you're reading a longish

Wikipedia entry is great, and working in Preview using the full screen lets you see more of the image you're tweaking.

Not every application has a Full Screen mode, but it's easy to figure out which ones can suck up all your screen real estate: look for the double arrows in the upper-right corner of the program's window (Figure 3-25).

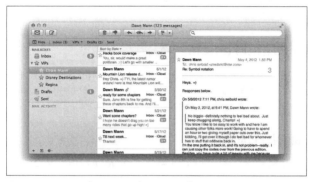

Figure 3-25. Mail is one of many Full Screen–capable apps in Mountain Lion

Once the application is in Full Screen mode, you can do whatever you wish, free from the distractions of your desktop and other programs. When you're using that application, move your cursor to the top of the screen and the menu bar will reappear. Click the blue arrows on the right end of the menu bar to return the program to a regular window.

You may be thinking that full-screen applications *seem* like a great idea but that they might be a little too much work when you need to use another program or get back to the desktop. Don't worry, there are plenty of easy ways to get out of a full-screen application. You can switch programs with the ⌘-Tab key combo, hit the Esc key to exit Full Screen mode, or invoke "Mission Control" on page 192.

NOTE

If you use multiple monitors, you might be hoping for a world where you can run one application in Full Screen mode while doing something else on the other monitor. Sadly, you're out of luck: launching a full-screen application in Mountain Lion renders the second monitor useless—unless your goal is to look at a static, gray-linen screen.

Files and Folders

As you already know, folders are where you keep files. But OS X also includes two special kinds of folders: Burn folders and Smart folders. This section explains 'em all.

Regular Folders

Your Mac comes preloaded with some folders that are appropriate for commonly saved files (documents, pictures, music, and so on), but you'll also want to make your own folders. For example, you might make a subfolder for spreadsheets within the Documents folder, or put a folder on your desktop where you can toss files that end up scattered around the desktop. To create a regular folder in the Finder, either choose File→New Folder (Shift-⌘-N), or right-click or Control-click a blank spot in a folder and then choose New Folder from the Context menu shown in Figure 3-26. You can also right-click or Control-click the desktop and then choose New Folder to add a folder there.

OS X names new folders "untitled folder," and it iterates this name if you create a series of folders without renaming them after you create each one, so you end up with "untitled folder," "untitled folder 2," "untitled folder 3," and so on. To change a folder's name, click the folder once and then press Return or click the folder's current name. The area surrounding the name gets highlighted so you can type a new one. When you're done, hit Return to make the new name stick.

Figure 3-26. Creating a new folder via the Context menu

Burn Folders

Creating a Burn folder is the easiest way to get files or folders from your Mac onto an optical disk (a CD or DVD). To do so, go to the Finder and select File→New Burn Folder; a new folder with a radiation symbol on it will appear in the current folder. (If you've made filename extensions visible—see "Finder preferences" on page 63—you'll notice that folder's suffix is *.fpbf*.) Be sure to give this folder a descriptive name like *discoinferno*. Then you can start tossing any files you want burned onto a disk into that folder.

The files aren't actually being moved to the Burn folder; Mountain Lion is just creating aliases that point to them; when the time comes to burn the data, OS X will burn the original file(s). Since the files are aliased, if you decide to get rid of the Burn folder without burning the data, you can simply toss the folder into the Trash. The original items will remain untouched.

Once you're ready to burn the data, open the Burn folder and click the Burn button in its upper-right corner. Insert a disk when prompted, and Mountain Lion takes care of the rest.

Smart Folders

There are Smart folders all over your Mac: in iTunes, Mail, and lots of other places. Smart folders are actually Spotlight search results, but you can browse them just like regular folders.

To create your own Smart folders, head to the Finder and choose File→New Smart Folder or press Option-⌘-N. In the search box of the new window that appears, type in text describing what you want to find, and Mountain Lion will fill the folder with items that meet your criteria. As you type, Mountain Lion displays suggestions for refining your search. Say you want an easy way to manage all your Word files. Start typing **.doc** in the search box, and Mountain Lion will make handy suggestions like the ones shown in Figure 3-27. Select "Word Document" under Kinds and all your Word documents will appear in the Smart folder.

Figure 3-27. OS X knows what you're looking for!

If the results aren't quite what you want, you can further refine your search by clicking the gear icon in the window's toolbar and selecting Show Search Criteria. Doing so will let you refine your search by adding more conditions for a match. (Love the search you created? Click Save and the search will be available to you anytime you need it.)

There are more great things about Smart folders. The results of your search don't change where anything is actually stored on your Mac, but you can act as if all the files reside in the Smart folder. That means that, even though the files in it could be scattered across a hundred folders on your Mac, you can move, copy, and delete them just as if they all resided in the Smart folder. (If you delete a file from a Smart folder, you'll also delete that file from your Mac.)

Don't worry about your Smart folders slowing down your Mac or not displaying changes immediately. Smart folders are constantly updated, so when you add a new file that fits the Smart folder's criteria, the file shows up in the Smart folder right away.

Nonessential (but Useful) OS X Features

Some features of Mountain Lion are really useful but not strictly required for day-to-day use. Spotlight is fantastic for searching your Mac, but some folks never need to search because they have insanely good organizational skills. Mission Control lets you see everything on your desktop (and more) at the same time—a lifesaver for those who work with multiple windows. If you're interested in one or more of these features, this is the place to look.

Sharing (Almost) Everywhere

One of the big changes in Mountain Lion is that it gives you the ability to share things easily and in multiple ways. Mountain Lion accomplishes this by adding a feature called Share Sheets to most applications. You access Share Sheets by clicking the Share button, which doesn't always look *exactly* the same (it matches the app you're using), but it resembles Figure 3-28.

When you see that icon, it means you can share whatever you're looking at with the world. Click the Share button and see your options for spreading the word about your new favorite thing. Figure 3-29 shows how you can share an image from Photo Booth.

Figure 3-28. The Share button (and Trash icon) in Notes

Figure 3-29. Photo Booth offers a ton of sharing options

NOTE

Before you'll get options to share on Twitter, you have to sign into Twitter. Once Mountain Lion sees you accessing Twitter, it'll ask if you want it to remember your Twitter info. If you choose Yes, the system will add Twitter to your Share Sheets (where applicable).

The exact options you see on the Share Sheet depend on the app you're using: The ways you can share something from Notes are different from the ways you can share something from Safari, for example. (See Figure 3-30.)

Even the information you can share differs depending on the share methods you choose. If you decide to email a web page to some friends, for example, the result will be an email message with the contents of that web page; it will look something like Figure 3-31.

Figure 3-30. Sharing a web page from Safari

Figure 3-31. Sharing a subtle present suggestion

If you choose to share the same web page via Messages instead, you'll just send the link to the recipients. If you opt to send the page to your followers using Twitter, you'll send out something that looks like Figure 3-32 and have the option to add your location.

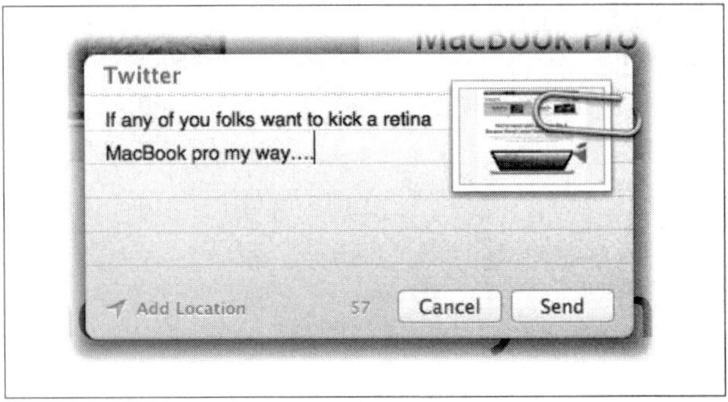

Figure 3-32. Tweeting a link

Not every app can share, though. Apps included with Mountain Lion that can share include Notes, Reminders, iPhoto, Photo Booth (you can even change your Twitter picture directly from Photo Booth), Safari, and FaceTime. And sharing isn't limited to apps created by Apple—other developers will be able to use the new sharing options built into Mountain Lion, too. To figure out whether an app can share, just look for the Share button.

Auto Save and Versions

Auto Save and Versions were introduced in Lion. Auto Save does exactly what its name implies: as you work on a document, song, movie, or whatever, Auto Save automatically saves your progress incrementally so you don't have to. Working in TextEdit and just want to quit? You don't need to save before quitting—Auto Save will save your work without being told to.

Versions are the result of all those saves. With Versions, if there's a change you want to undo, you aren't stuck with the most recent version of your file. Use TextEdit as an example. Once you create a document and start typing in it, the word "Edited" appears in the title bar to let you know that Auto Save is working. Click Edited to reveal a drop-down menu that gives you six options:

Rename...

> You can guess what this does: it lets you give the document you're working on a new name.

Move To...

> Lets you choose where you want to save the document. iCloud is an option, naturally.

Duplicate

> Choosing this option lets you create a copy of the current version of the file you're working on and save it to a new location.

Lock

> This option lets you lock the document. Once it's locked, you won't be able to edit it, but you can use it as a template for a new document. Think of this as a way of being sure you don't make any boneheaded changes to something you worked long and hard to create.

Last Saved

> Choosing this item reverts to the last version you explicitly saved with the Save command (not the latest version that Auto Save created).

Browse All Versions

> This is where Versions comes in. If you've made some changes to your file that you like and some that you hate, you can use Versions to pick out the moment in time when your file was at its best. Select this option from the drop-down menu and you'll see a screen reminiscent of Time Machine. You can then flip through the incremental changes Mountain Lion has been tracking and pick out the version you like the most.

WARNING

Not every application works with Auto Save, so don't depend on Auto Save to back up your work unless you're *sure* the program you're using supports it.

Auto Save and Versions work with iCloud as well, so if you've saved your document to iCloud it is automatically updated on the cloud.

Searching with Spotlight

Using Spotlight is easy: Simply click the magnifying glass icon in the upper-right corner of your screen and start typing the name of the item you're looking for.

In Snow Leopard, Spotlight lets you search through only the files on your computer. But these days, it also lets you search the Web or Wikipedia, as shown in Figure 3-33. (The results will open with OS X's Dictionary application.) You also get Quick Look previews: just highlight the most promising-looking results and Quick Look will give you a detailed look at the file or web page. Plus, you can drag and drop things directly from Spotlight. Found that GarageBand file you want to send to your pal? Drag it right to AirDrop to make the process quick and painless.

When it's searching your computer, Spotlight works by indexing (making a list of) all the files on your Mac according to the files' metadata and contents. So if you type "Lake Monsters Stole My Thursday" into a document, that bit of data will be available to Spotlight. The moment you type "lake monsters stole" into Spotlight's search field, you'll see a list of matching files. By the time you've typed the entire string into Spotlight, the document where you wrote it will be the top result.

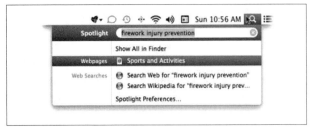

Figure 3-33. Choose where you want your results to come from

About Metadata

Metadata is information about a file. This includes obvious things like the date it was created and its file type, as well as a lot of unexpected info. An image's metadata, for example, contains information about its size, pixel count, and so on. Spotlight is smart enough to realize that when you're searching, you're most likely searching for a particular file's name or contents, as opposed to more esoteric metadata. So, while Spotlight indexes everything (unless you tell it not to—see below), it puts results like documents and folders higher on its lists of results than more obscure matches (unless you change the order of its results—see below). That way, you won't be burdened by information overload when performing Spotlight searches.

Changing the order of Spotlight's results

You can adjust how Spotlight arranges its results either by choosing ■→System Preferences→Spotlight→Search Results or clicking Spotlight Preferences at the bottom of any list of Spotlight search results. In the window that appears, drag the categories into your preferred order.

Controlling the results Spotlight displays

If you don't want your Spotlight search results cluttered with stuff you're not interested in, go to ■→System Preferences→Spotlight→Search Results and uncheck the boxes next to any categories you find less than compelling. Be aware that not returning results from certain categories doesn't mean those files aren't indexed; read on to learn how to control *what* Spotlight indexes.

Controlling what Spotlight indexes

There are some things you just don't want indexed: your plans for world domination, your Pog value spreadsheet, and so forth. To keep the things you want private out of Spotlight's index, go to →System Preferences→Spotlight→Privacy. Clicking the + button brings up a file-browsing window where you can select things you want to keep Spotlight from indexing. You can exclude folders or entire disks. Unfortunately, you can't exclude a single file, so if you're trying to keep just one file out of the index, you either have to exclude the folder it's in (along with all of the folder's other contents) or move it into its own folder and exclude that.

Managing File Info

As you learned above, Spotlight works by indexing metadata. What if you want to add some metadata so Spotlight can find files or folders with greater precision? The Info window is your key to adding metadata (and changing other things, too). To open an item's Info window, select the item in the Finder and then either select File→Get Info or press ⌘-I. The window that appears will look something like Figure 3-34.

This window has several subsections:

Spotlight comments
> Spotlight will index anything you type here and use it when it searches.

General
> This section includes pertinent data about the file (if this section is collapsed, click the disclosure triangle next to the word "General"). If you check the "Stationery pad" box (which appears only when applicable), the file turns into a read-only file, meaning you can look at it and save it as a new file, but you can't save it with the same name as the Stationery pad; this effectively turns the file into a template. If you're constantly tweaking the same document, you can use the template you created by checking the Stationery pad box as a starting point. (For example, if you are constantly generating TPS reports but you change only the last page, you can mark the document as a Stationery pad. You can then open it and add what you need to without worrying about corrupting the master

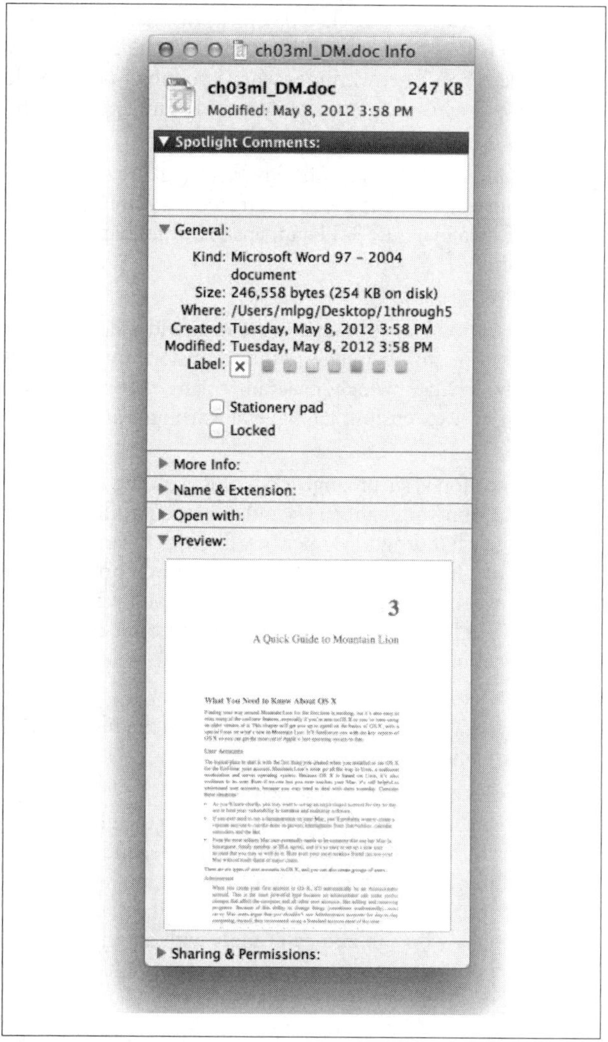

Figure 3-34. Get Info is a very useful window

file.) Checking the Locked box locks the file. A locked file is much like a Stationery Pad except you can't easily throw it away. You'll get warnings when you move a locked file to the Trash and again when you go to empty the Trash.

More Info

Clicking the More Info disclosure triangle reveals where the file originated if it wasn't created on your Mac. (The file shown in Figure 3-34 happens to be the chapter you're reading.)

Name & Extension

This section lets you rename the item and hide its extension. You can also change the extension, but that will (likely) change which program opens the file. If you change the extension, you'll get a warning from OS X.

Open with

This section is surprisingly powerful. You can choose the application you want to open this particular file with, or change what programs open any file with the same extension by clicking Change All. Clicking the pop-up menu will reveal suggested choices, but if you don't want to trust OS X's advice, you can select Other to force a different application to open that file.

Preview

This section shows the same preview of the file that you see when using the Finder.

Sharing & Permissions

This is where you can fine-tune access to the file. The options you're first presented with differ depending on the file, but generally include your account, an admin, and everyone. Those are usually enough, but if you *really* want to control who can and can't mess with a particular file, click the + button to bring up even more options, as shown in Figure 3-35.

In the window that appears, you can grant access to specific individuals. Note that adding someone new (from your Address Book, for instance) will bring up a dialog

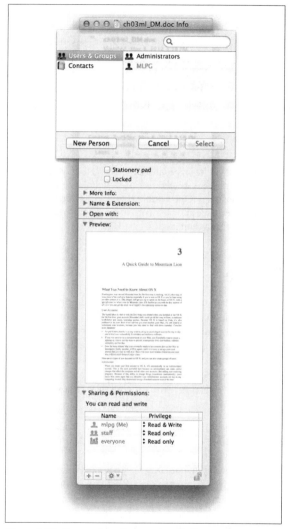

Figure 3-35. Fine-tuning who can share a file

box where you can set a password for the item, and will add a Sharing account to your Mac for that person. Adding a new group of people will add a new Group account.

Finally, if you've made a bunch of changes to sharing and then thought better of it, you can click the gear icon at the bottom of the Info window and then undo what you've wrought by selecting "Revert changes."

NOTE

The Sharing & Permissions section also includes a lock icon. If you're logged in as a Standard user, you can click it to unlock restricted features, such as the Change All button in the "Open with" section. However, you'll need the username and password of an administrative user to make those changes.

Resume

When you use an app on an iOS device, the app starts up right where you left off the last time you ran it. Mountain Lion can do this, too, thanks to Resume. If you quit Safari with 10 windows open, those same windows will pop open when you restart Safari. Resume also works when you shut down or log out: when you restart or log back in, all the apps you were using automatically relaunch and open all the windows you had open before.

Resume works just like it did in Lion, which is great if you liked Resume. Unfortunately, Resume is one of those love-it-or-hate-it deals. If you're in love-it camp, you don't have anything to worry about. If you hate it, you can make your Mac much more tolerable with just a few steps. First you'll want to make your Mac close windows when quitting an app. Head to →System Preferences→General, and then check the box next to "Close windows when quitting an application." This will keep Mountain Lion from restoring open windows when you relaunch an application, but it won't keep Mountain Lion from reopening all the apps you had running the last time you logged in when you log back in, and that can be annoying, too. To make your Mac start without restarting every app you had running when you logged out, make sure the checkbox shown in Figure 3-36 is unchecked (the dialog box in Figure 3-36 pops up when you log out).

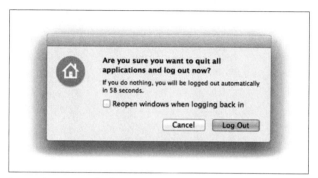

Figure 3-36. Keep this box unchecked if you hate having apps auto-start

CHAPTER 4

Troubleshooting OS X

OS X is a robust operating system; while problems are rare, they do show up from time to time. Since these issues always seem to present themselves at the worst possible moment, it helps if you know the best ways to troubleshoot them. That's what this chapter is all about, and it's a great reason to keep this book in your pocket!

Common Problems

There are a lot of things that can go wrong with your Mac: Hardware problems, software glitches, and configuration issues can happen at any moment. Most of the problems you'll encounter can be easily addressed or diagnosed by following the steps in this chapter.

However, some issues are unusual or won't respond to the fixes listed in this chapter. A great resource for those situations is Apple's website: *www.apple.com/support*. As you'd expect, you can browse manuals and tutorials on that site. More useful when trying to fix that quirky problem, though, are the communities you can access via that site, where you'll likely find someone who's having the same problem you are—and the fix.

If the information there doesn't resolve things, you could have a unique issue, in which case a trip to your local Apple Store or a call to Apple is in order. You can find a complete list of technical support numbers for Apple at *www.apple.com/support/contact/phone_contacts.html*. In the United States, the number is 1-800-275-2273.

Misbehaving Applications

One of the most common problems on a Mac is an application that isn't behaving as expected. This issue comes in many forms: an application that unexpectedly quits repeatedly, stops responding, or just doesn't perform the way it normally does. This section suggests ways to resolve all these issues and more.

An application stops responding

Occasionally, an application will simply stop reacting to anything. Your mouse or trackpad will still work, and other programs will be fine, but if you want to use the troublesome program, all you'll get is a spinning beach-ball cursor (instead of the mouse pointer) and you'll have no way to input anything.

Don't panic—there's an easy fix. Simply right-click or Control-click the stalled application's icon in the Dock to bring up its Dock menu (Figure 4-1). If you see Application Not Responding in faint text at the top of the menu, you'll also see a Force Quit option. Select Force Quit and OS X will kill the program.

You may also need another way to kill applications, because occasionally a program can become unresponsive without OS X realizing that the program is in peril. For these times, launch the Force Quit Applications dialog box either by selecting ＄→Force Quit or using the key combo Option-⌘-Esc. You can also try holding down Shift as you click the ＄ menu, then select "Force Quit [application name]" to kill the frontmost application.

There's some good news when it comes to force quitting applications in Mountain Lion. In the old days of OS X (before Lion), any changes you made between the last time you saved a document and the moment the application started misbehaving were gone forever. But thanks to Auto Save, if you're forced to quit an application, Mountain Lion preserves the work you've done since the last time you manually saved.

Figure 4-1. Force quitting Safari

WARNING

"Save early, save often" is still good advice, since Auto Save works only with applications specifically built with Auto Save in mind. That means that work you do in apps designed for Lion or Mountain Lion will be saved, but applications that haven't been updated since Lion came out *won't* automatically save your work.

The Finder stops responding

The Finder is just another program, so it can get hung up, too. If that happens, either head to →Force Quit or use the key combination ⌘-Option-Esc. If nothing happens, try clicking the Dock or some other application first, and *then* use the menu or ⌘-Option-Esc to invoke the Force Quit dialog box.

NOTE

When you select an application in the Force Quit dialog box, the dialog box's button reads "Force Quit." However, if you select the Finder, the button reads "Relaunch" instead. Why? Unlike every other application, the Finder will be restarted immediately after it's forced to quit.

Force quitting greedy processes

If you suspect something is eating up too much processor time or hogging too many system resources (because your Mac is running really slowly, say, or the fans are running at full speed for no obvious reason), Force Quit won't help you figure out which application is the culprit. Instead, open Activity Monitor (Applications→Utilities→Activity Monitor), click its CPU tab in the lower half of the window, and then look for any processes that are using a lot of CPU resources for more than a few seconds. (Safari and its helper applications occasionally do this, particularly with runaway Flash or JavaScript code.) When you identify a suspect, single-click the renegade process's name and then click the big red Quit Process button (you can't miss it—it's shaped like a stop sign).

WARNING

Be careful which applications you quit in this way. There are some programs that your Mac runs in the background, and many of these are important in helping your computer operate normally. Here's a rule of thumb: if you don't recognize the name of the program as an application that you launched, don't kill it. Instead, do a Google search on its name (for good measure, include the terms "OS X" and "cpu," too). Chances are good you'll find a solution for whatever is causing that process to use up so much CPU time.

USB device problems

It seems like computers never have enough USB ports, so most of us end up using USB hubs (or keyboards that have extra USB ports). Then we plug some fantastic new USB device into the hub—and it doesn't work. In fact, if you dig through System Information (it's in the /Applications/Utilities folder) and look at the USB Device Tree (click USB in the list on the left), the hub shows up, but not the device.

Often the problem is that the device requires a *powered* USB port and you're using an unpowered hub (or you've maxed out the power capabilities of the hub or port). Switching to a powered hub might fix the problem, but that isn't guaranteed. What works most often is plugging the device directly into your Mac, which means you'll need to shuffle your various USB devices around. If any of them can run off of their own external power supply rather than taking power from the USB port, that may help as well (sometimes these power supplies are sold separately; check with the device's manufacturer).

The second method of attacking USB device problems is a little more involved. First, shut down your Mac and unplug all the USB devices (even the ones that use external power supplies). Reboot your Mac, and then plug them back in one at a time while watching the USB Device Tree (it's updated quickly so you'll see each device appear as it's plugged in) to figure out which device isn't playing nicely with others. Sometimes going through this process results in all the devices suddenly working. But if you discover that only a certain device isn't working, the fix may be to install a new driver for it. Check the manufacturer's website for updates.

Battery problems

MacBook users are faced with a problem that desktop users don't have to worry about: the battery. The goal of most Apple batteries is to still provide 80% of the original charge capacity after a certain number of cycles (charges and discharges). The number of cycles varies depending on your machine. For

Mountain Lion–capable MacBooks, the cycle count is either 750 or 1,000 cycles (depending on the model). If you notice your battery isn't holding a charge for as long as it used to, the first thing to do is launch System Information (Applications→Utilities→System Information) and then click Power in the list on the left; see Figure 4-2.

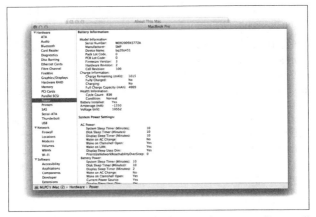

Figure 4-2. The Power section of System Information tells you all about your battery

The Battery Information list includes your battery's full charge capacity, how many cycles it's been through, and its condition. If the condition is listed as Replace Soon or something equally ominous, it's time to think about getting a new battery. If the cycle count is low but the battery is *still* running out of juice prematurely, here are a couple of things you can try:

Calibrate the battery

Inside every MacBook battery is a microcontroller that tells your computer how long the battery is going to last until it runs out of juice. Over time, this estimation can get further and further from real-world performance. To get the computer and the microcontroller on the same page, you need to recalibrate the battery from time to time. To do so, fully charge the battery and then keep your computer plugged into the power adapter for two more hours. Next, unplug the power adapter and fully drain the battery. When a warning pops up alerting you that the battery is running dangerously low, save your work and keep on trucking until your computer automatically goes to sleep. Then let the computer sleep for more than five hours to make sure every drop of power is gone. Finally, plug in the power adapter and let your computer fully charge. The battery indicator should now be successfully recalibrated.

NOTE

If your MacBook has an internal battery, Apple recommends *not* calibrating the battery because these internal batteries should be serviced only by an authorized repair center.

Reset the SMC

SMC is short for the System Management Controller, a chip that's responsible for hard drive spin-down, sleeping your Mac, waking your Mac, and keyboard backlighting. A malfunctioning SMC can prevent the battery from charging, so you need to reset the SMC. How you do that depends on whether your MacBook has an internal battery (like all the newer MacBooks) or a battery that you can easily remove. If it has a removable battery, shut it down, unplug the power adapter from the wall and the computer, and then remove the battery. Next, press the power button for five seconds. After that, replace the battery, plug in the power adapter, and then restart the computer. If your MacBook has an internal battery, shut down the computer and plug it into an adapter that's getting power. On the left side of the keyboard, hold down Left Shift-Control-Option, and then press the power button. Keep all these buttons depressed (including the power button) for five seconds and then release them all simultaneously. Pat yourself on the back for pulling off an impressive feat of manual dexterity, and then press the power button to restart the computer.

If those remedies don't restore your battery, it's likely time for a trip to the local Apple Store or authorized repair center. If your computer is under warranty and your cycle count is low, Apple will probably replace the battery for free. If your cycle count is over the recommended number and the performance degradation is within expectations, you'll probably need to pay for a new battery or live with the reduced (and ever-shrinking) battery capacity.

NOTE

Like many computer makers, Apple has had its share of battery recalls, both for safety and performance reasons. So check with Apple to see if your battery is under recall. If so, it's likely that it will replace the battery even if your computer is out of warranty.

Display problems

Most Macs come with a built-in display that doesn't require special configuration, so display problems are uncommon. When they do happen, they're often caused by user error. The fix, while usually easy, isn't readily apparent. Here are some things to try:

Fuzzy/tiny display

If your display is fuzzy or everything is suddenly bigger than you remember, it's possible that someone changed the display's resolution (on some systems, this may also manifest itself as a small screen with black bars around its edges). Head to →System Preferences→Displays and look for the monitor's native resolution (on Macs with built-in displays, this is usually the highest resolution available—the one at the top of the list). Once you select the optimal resolution, things should look normal again.

Your display moves with your mouse

The weird thing is that this always happens when children under five are on your lap while you're using your computer. Is there some kind of kid detector in your Mac that causes this? Nope—your kid just pressed some keys while you were working. (If you don't have kids or lap cats, then it was probably you.)

There are a couple of key combinations that will cause your Mac to zoom the screen. The most common is holding down Control while you zoom in or out with your mouse or trackpad. Once you're zoomed in, your mouse will suddenly start dragging the screen around, which is disconcerting if you aren't expecting it. To turn it off, hold down Control and zoom out with your trackpad or mouse wheel.

There are a couple of other key sequences that can be invoked accidentally: Option-⌘-8 toggles keyboard zooming on and off, and holding down = or – while pressing Option-⌘ zooms in or out, respectively.

Startup Problems

A misbehaving application is bad enough, but a Mac that won't start properly is truly disconcerting. The good news is that most such problems are repairable. The general method of attack in this case is to get your Mac to a state where you can run Disk Utility and repair the drive. However, there are some situations where you can't even get to that point.

Your Mac beeps instead of starting

If your Mac just beeps at you when you try to start it up, it's trying to tell you something: one beep means there's no memory (RAM) installed, and three beeps means your RAM doesn't pass the integrity check. The problem could be a bad RAM module, so you'll need to open up your Mac and replace the module.

Try installing some memory that you're certain is fully functional to see if that resolves the problem. If you don't have any spare memory lying around, try removing all the RAM modules and then replacing them one by one until you've isolated the bad module.

NOTE

If you don't know how to replace memory in your Mac, check the user guide that came with it. Or if your Mac is still under warranty, just take it into an Apple Store for service.

Your hard drive is making noises

If you suspect you've got a physical hard drive problem, you need to check things out quickly before they get much, much worse. If you hear a strange noise coming from your machine, that's an obvious sign of a hard drive problem, but these issues can also be indicated by the computer stalling for several seconds at a time (or making a clicking sound when stalling).

Just as with a car, when a bad sound is emanating from your hard drive, it's usually a bad thing. If you've ever listened to National Public Radio's *Car Talk*, you know that one of the highlights is when callers try to imitate the sounds their cars are making. If you're inclined to try identifying your hard drive's sound by ear, head over to *http://datacent.com/hard_drive_sounds.php* and take a listen to the sounds of dying drives, sorted by manufacturer.

WARNING

If your hard drive is failing, you're likely to lose more data every moment it's running. If you don't have current backups, your best bet is to replace the drive immediately and either seek a data-recovery professional or, if you don't have the money for that, install the damaged drive in an external drive enclosure and use the GNU ddrescue utility (*www.gnu.org/software/ddrescue*) to recover the data on the damaged drive.

If you aren't hearing any unusual sounds but still suspect your hard drive is causing your problems, head to Disk Utility (Applications→Utilities→Disk Utility) and check the S.M.A.R.T. status of the drive. (Using a computer means loving acronyms, and this time the acronym is clever, if a little forced: S.M.A.R.T. stands for Self-Monitoring Analysis and Reporting Technology.)

NOTE

S.M.A.R.T. isn't available on every drive, so if you don't see this option, don't worry!

The idea behind S.M.A.R.T. is that many hard disk failures are predictable and computer users, if given a heads-up that their hard drive is on the verge of failing, will be able to recover data *before* the failure actually happens. You can find your drive's S.M.A.R.T. status by opening Disk Utility and selecting the disk you're worried about in the list on the left. In the lower-right part of the Disk Utility window, you'll see the S.M.A.R.T. Status (Figure 4-3): either Verified (everything is fine) or "About to Fail." If you get the "About to Fail" notice, don't waste any time: if your Mac is under warranty, take it into an Apple Store; otherwise, back up your data as soon as possible and start pricing out a new drive.

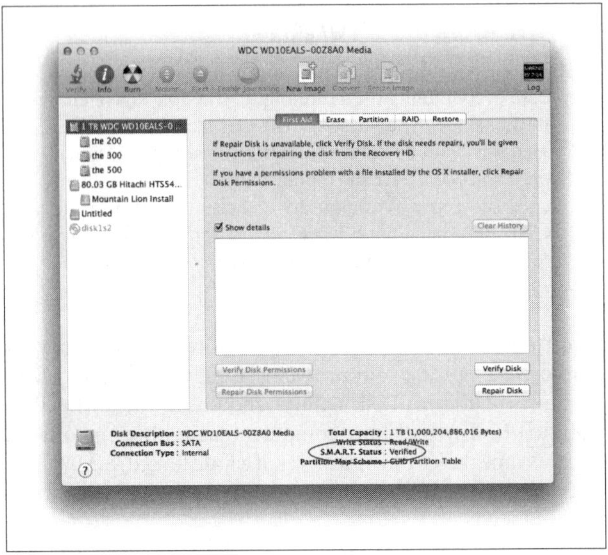

Figure 4-3. "Verified" means this drive is fine

WARNING

S.M.A.R.T. isn't perfect (that's no surprise—nothing is). You can have a problematic drive that S.M.A.R.T. won't recognize. So if you're having consistent problems and S.M.A.R.T. keeps telling you everything is fine, don't discount the drive as the source of the problems after you've exhausted other fixes.

Startup troubleshooting

Thankfully, the hardware failures just described are relatively rare. Much more common are software failures: corrupt files, wonky login items, and even font problems can cause a startup failure. These issues are generally repairable, hopefully without data loss. Unfortunately, when you have one of these problems, the cause isn't immediately obvious. When faced with a

Mac that won't boot, there are a few things you can try to get your computer back to a usable state:

Restart your Mac

A lot happens when OS X starts up: it checks your Mac's hardware, prepares the system software, and more. During the startup process, there are ample opportunities for something to go wrong, especially right after you install an update to OS X or even an application. If your Mac won't complete the startup sequence, don't panic; simply restart the machine by holding down the power button until you hear a chime; chances are everything will be fine.

WARNING

If you see a flashing question mark when you try to start your Mac, it means that your machine can't find its startup disk. In that case, skip ahead to "Restart in Recovery Mode" later in this list.

Safe Boot

If a simple restart doesn't do the trick, it means you have problems that persist across restarts, so the next step is a Safe Boot. In Safe Mode, all your Mac's startup items are disabled, font caches are cleared, and some other potentially problematic items are avoided. More important, Safe Boot gives you a chance to run Disk Utility, uninstall any software that may be misbehaving, or back up your data before whatever is causing the problem gets worse. To boot your Mac in Safe Mode, restart it while holding the Shift key. Once you see a progress bar appear on the lower half of the screen, you can release the Shift key and your Mac will boot in Safe Mode. Once it has booted, run Disk Utility (Applications→Utilities→Disk Utility).

NOTE

When you're booting in Safe Mode, the Login window automatically appears even if you usually use Automatic Login. Don't be alarmed by the change—it's a sign that Safe Mode is working as expected.

Restart in Recovery Mode

Before Lion, one remedy to try when your Mac went bad was to boot from the DVD you either got with your Mac or purchased when you upgraded to Snow Leopard. But since you don't use any physical media—DVD or otherwise—when you install Mountain Lion, this trick doesn't work anymore. Fortunately, Apple realizes that, when problems occur, you might need to boot your Mac from a different source than usual, so Mountain Lion includes Recovery Mode.

NOTE

You need to be connected to the Internet to use Recovery Mode to reinstall Mountain Lion. The Reinstall Mountain Lion option will download every byte of the Mountain Lion installer, so you might want to try other fixes before going through that process.

Recovery Mode lets you boot from a virtual partition called Recovery 10.8. When you boot into Recovery Mode, you'll find yourself running a special system that lets you restore your Mac from a Time Machine backup, reinstall Mountain Lion, use Safari to look for solutions to your problem online, or run Disk Utility. (Don't be afraid to launch Safari even if you're not connected to the Internet; there's a static web page with basic instructions that automatically opens when you launch the program.)

NOTE

You can only run one application at a time in Recovery Mode, so if you're running Disk Utility, say, you can't also launch Safari. Being aware of this limitation can save you some frustration and endless restarts.

In addition to Recovery Mode's obvious choices, you can also run Firmware Password Utility, Network Utility, and Terminal by visiting the Utilities drop-down menu at the top of the screen. With all of these options, you'll likely find one that can fix your Mac woes.

To boot in Recovery Mode, hold down the Option key while starting your Mac (this process should be familiar if you've booted Macs from alternative disks before). You'll be presented with a screen that shows all the viable startup partitions available. Double-click Recovery-10.8, and you'll be well on your way to diagnosing (and hopefully fixing) whatever problem is currently plaguing your Mac.

NOTE

If you have a brand-new Mac (one that came with Mountain Lion installed), you have one more trick you can use: Internet Recovery. If something terrible happens to your machine (a massive hard drive failure, say) or you want to install Mountain Lion onto a completely blank hard drive, hold down the Option key while starting your Mac, and then choose Internet Recovery. Once you tell your computer which network to use, it will boot from Apple's servers. Once booted, your Mac will download the Recovery 10.8 image from Apple. After that, the process is the same as for a standard Mountain Lion reinstall.

This section emphasized tools that come with Mountain Lion because, well, if you've installed Mountain Lion, you have access to them. But these tools aren't the only ones available when things go wrong. There are several disk repair programs (many of which are more powerful than Disk Utility) from third parties, such as DiskWarrior (*www.alsoft.com/DiskWarrior*) and TechTool Pro (*www.micromat.com*).

Reset your PRAM

This maneuver gets its own section only because it's one of the oldest troubleshooting techniques in Mac history.

PRAM (parameter random access memory) is where your Mac stores many of its hardware settings. Resetting the PRAM almost never resolves a startup issue, but it's something Apple support usually asks you to do when troubleshooting a problem (and it does, in some rare cases, help). To reset the PRAM, turn on your Mac, *immediately* press and hold Option-⌘-P-R, and continue to hold those keys until your Mac restarts and you hear the startup chime a total of three times. After you do this, you may have to reconfigure some of the system settings (like date, time, and possibly keyboard/mouse settings if you've customized them).

CHAPTER 5

System Preferences

Out of the box, the Mac is a fantastic machine. Its graphical interface is clean and uncluttered, you can use it to accomplish tasks with a minimum of frustration, and everything performs exactly how you expect it to. That honeymoon lasts for somewhere between 10 seconds and a week. While everything is great at first, you'll soon find yourself saying, "Man, it sure would be better if...." When this happens, your first stop should be System Preferences.

Apple knows that different people want different behaviors from their Macs. While Mountain Lion can't possibly accommodate everything that everyone might want to do, most of the changes you're likely to want to make are built right into Mountain Lion.

System Preferences, which you can get to by clicking the silver-framed gears icon in the Dock (unless you've removed it from the Dock, in which case you can find it in the Applications folder or the menu), is the place to make your Mac uniquely yours. But as you'll see later in this chapter, you can also make some tweaks by going beyond System Preferences.

One thing that will inevitably happen while you're adjusting your System Preferences is that you'll make a change and later decide that it was a mistake. For example, say you adjust the time it takes for your Mac to go to sleep and later decide that

Apple had it right out of the box. Fortunately, some preference panes feature a Restore Defaults button that resets the settings in that particular pane to the factory defaults.

Mountain Lion comes with 29 preference panes, each of which controls a bevy of related preferences. With all those options, how will you remember where to find every setting? For example, are the settings for display sleep under Energy Saver or Displays? Mountain Lion makes it easy to find the right preference pane by including a search box right in the System Preferences window (OS X is big on search boxes). Type in what you're looking for; the likely choices get highlighted, and you'll see a list of suggested searches (Figure 5-1).

Figure 5-1. Likely candidates for keyboard-related preferences

---

NOTE

Try searching for one term at a time. For example, if you can't find the settings for putting your display to sleep by searching for "display sleep," try searching for "display" or "sleep" instead.

Preference Pane Rundown

With so many preference panes, it's hard to keep track of what they all do. This section describes each one.

The System Preferences window is divided into five categories: Personal, Hardware, Internet & Wireless, System, and Other. However, you may see only the first four because the Other category is reserved for non-Apple preference panes and doesn't appear until you've installed at least one third-party preference pane (which usually, but not always, is part of a third-party application).

Some preferences, such as those that affect all users of the computer, need to be unlocked before you can tweak them. (If a preference pane is locked, there will be a lock icon in its lower left.) These can be unlocked only by a user who has administrative access. On most Macs, the first user you create has those privileges. If you don't have administrative privileges, you'll need to find the person who *does* and have him or her type in the username and password before you can make changes.

General

This preference pane lets you tweak the look and feel of OS X. The first two options control colors. The Appearance setting controls the overall look of buttons, menus, and windows and has two choices: blue or gray. The Highlight setting controls the color used for text you've selected and offers more choices, including selecting your own color (choose Other). And the "Sidebar icon size" setting lets you adjust, well, the size of the icons in OS X's various sidebars. (The most obvious sidebar is in the Finder, but if you adjust this setting, other sidebars—like Mail's—will also change.)

The second section of this pane lets you decide when you want the scroll bar to show up. "Automatically based on mouse or trackpad" leaves the decision up to your Mac; "When scrolling" means the bars show up only when you're actively scrolling; and, for those who long for the days of Snow Leopard, "Always" keeps them visible all the time. No matter which option you choose, you're stuck with gray scroll bars—no more colorful scrolling.

You'll also find options to modify what happens when you click a scroll bar. You can set it to automatically jump to the next page or to the spot that you clicked. The difference between these options isn't trivial: if you're looking at a lengthy web page or a 1,000-page document, opting for "Jump to next page" means it'll take a lot of clicks to reach the end, whereas "Jump to the spot that's clicked" could shoot all the way to the end in a flash.

By default, Mountain Lion shows your 10 most recent applications, documents, and servers in the menu's Recent Items submenu, but you can change that number here.

Desktop & Screen Saver

The Desktop & Screen Saver preference pane has two tabs. The Desktop tab lets you change the desktop background (also known as wallpaper). You can use the Apple-supplied images, solid colors (click Custom Color to create your own), or pictures from your iPhoto library. You can even specify a whole folder of images by clicking the + button in the tab's lower-left corner.

NOTE

If you're using multiple monitors and invoke this preference pane, your Mac will open one window on each monitor. You guessed it: this lets you control the desktop picture and color for each monitor individually!

If you pick an image of your own, you can control how it's displayed by selecting Fill Screen, Fit to Screen, Stretch to Fill Screen, Center, or Tile from the menu to the right of the image preview. If you like a little liveliness, you can tell your computer to change the desktop picture periodically. Apple supplies options ranging from every five seconds to every time you log in or wake from sleep. And if you want your menu bar to be solid instead of see-through, turn off the "Translucent menu bar" checkbox.

WARNING

If you choose to change the picture periodically without carefully vetting the source images, you'll likely be presented with something completely useless, confusing, or embarrassing at a random moment.

The Screen Saver tab is a bit more complicated. In the left half of the pane, you'll find a long list of slideshows (14 different styles, to be exact). Select a slideshow style and, in the right side, you'll see a Source pop-up menu that lets you tell the slideshow to use images from one of four default collections (National Geographic, Aerial, Cosmos, Nature Patterns) that all look fantastic. You can also pick a folder for the slideshow to use. Finally you'll see a "Shuffle slide order" checkbox, which you should check if you grow tired of the same progression of pictures time after time.

If you scroll past the 14 slideshow options, you'll discover Screen Savers. Your choices are limited to only six option (seven if you count Random). Select the screen saver you want your Mac to use, and you're done. Well, maybe not—depending on the screen saver you choose, you might get options. If that is the case, the Screen Saver Options button in the right side of the pane becomes clickable. Clicking it lets you set options for that screen saver.

Below the area where you choose slideshows and screen savers, you'll find a pop-up menu labeled Start After which allows you to control how long your Mac is idle before displaying your chosen slideshow or screen saver. You'll also find a checkbox labeled "Show with clock," which makes your Mac display a clock with your chosen animation.

If you'd like the screensaver to kick in on demand—handy when you're messing around online and the boss walks in— you can set a *hot corner* that lets you invoke the screensaver right away. Click the Hot Corners button and you'll get a new window with options for every corner. Use the drop-down menus to set options for any corner you want. After that, when you move your mouse to that corner, your Mac fires up the screensaver (or does what you told it to—put the display to sleep, launch Mission Control, or whatever). The only downside of setting hot corners is that Apple gives you eight options for each corner, so unless you want to use a modifier key with the corner, you don't have enough corners to use all the options.

NOTE

By using modifier keys (you can choose from Shift, ⌘, Option, and Control), you can get a single corner to do many different things. To add a modifier key to a hot corner, hold down the modifier key while you select what you want the hot corner to do from the Active Screen Corners window's menus. Using modifiers with hot corners not only gives you extra flexibility, but it also prevents you from accidentally invoking the hot corner action when you're mousing around.

Dock

There aren't a lot of options in the Dock preference pane, but they give you control over the most important aspects of the Dock. You can change its size—from illegibly small to ridiculously large—with the aptly named Size slider, which works in real time so you can see the change as you're making it.

If you turn on Magnification, the application or document you're mousing over will become larger than the rest of the items in your Dock. How much larger? Use the Magnification slider to determine that.

If you want to move the Dock somewhere else, click one of the three "Position on screen" radio buttons: Left, Bottom, or Right. (Top isn't an option because you don't want the Dock to compete with the menu bar.)

The "Minimize windows using" menu lets you choose which animation your Mac uses when you minimize a window: the Genie or Scale effect. (These days, this is just a matter of personal preference, but in the early days of OS X, some machines weren't fast enough to render the Genie effect.) The "Double-click a window's title bar to minimize" checkbox does just what you'd think—with this setting turned on, you can minimize windows by double-clicking their title bars.

The "Minimize windows into application icon" setting determines where your windows go when you click the yellow button found at the upper left of almost every window. If you leave this unchecked, then minimized windows appear on the right side of the Dock (or at the bottom of it if you put the Dock on the left or right side of your screen). If you turn on this checkbox, you'll save space in the Dock, but to restore minimized application windows, you'll have to right-click or Control-click the appropriate application's icon in the Dock, select the minimized window from the application's window menu, or invoke Mission Control.

The checkbox labeled "Animate opening applications" sounds like more fun than it actually is. All it does is control whether applications' Dock icons bounce when you launch them. If you turn this option off, you'll still be able to tell when an application is starting because the dot that appears under it (or next to it, if the Dock is positioned on the left or right) will pulse (unless you've turned off the indicator lights, as explained in a sec). If you turn on "Automatically hide and show the Dock," it will remain hidden until you move the mouse above or next to it.

The blue dots in the Dock that indicate that an application is running really bother some people. If these dots are the bane of your existence, unchecking the "Show indicator lights for open applications" box to make them go away. To figure out which apps are running once you've banished the dots, use Mission Control or the Application Switcher.

Mission Control

This pane allows you to adjust how you invoke Mission Control and what happens when you do.

You'll find an option to display Dashboard as a desktop space, which is turned on by default; this setting puts a mini-sized Dashboard screen at the top of your monitor with your other spaces. You can opt to have OS X arrange your spaces so that the ones you've used most recently are at the top of the list; if you like to manually set your spaces, uncheck this option. You can also have OS X switch you to a space with an open window when you switch applications. With this option on (which it is by default), if you have a space with a Safari window open, say, and you switch to Safari from another space or full-screen application, the space you switch to will have a Safari window open already. If you turn this option off, you might find yourself in a space without an open window for the application you just switched to, which can be confusing. The final option, which is on by default, tells Mission Control whether to group windows by application. Leaving this box checked keeps all the windows for Safari (for example) together when you invoke Mission Control.

You also get to change the shortcuts for invoking Mission Control, opening application windows, showing the desktop, and showing the Dashboard. Finally, the Hot Corners button lets you define what your Mac does when you slide your cursor to a corner of the screen (everything from launching Mission Control to putting your display to sleep).

Language & Text

The Language tab of the Language & Text preference pane lets you set the language your Mac uses.

The Text tab is helpful if you spend much time typing. It includes a list of symbol and text substitutions your Mac performs, which lets you do things like type (r) and have it automatically show up as ®. Even better, you can add your *own* substitutions. Click the + button below the list to add whatever text you want substituted and what you want it replaced with; make sure the checkbox to its left is turned on, and your Mac should make that fix automatically from then on. This won't work in every application, but in the supported ones, text substitutions can save you a lot of effort.

The Text tab also lets you adjust how OS X checks spelling (the default is automatic by language, but you can have it check everything for French even if your Mac is using English). The Word Break setting affects how words are selected when you double-click on a word, and two drop-down menus let you customize how double and single quotes are formatted.

The Region tab (which, before Mountain Lion, was called the Format tab) lets you control the format of the date, time, and numbers on your machine; pick which currency symbol to use; and choose between US (imperial) and metric units of measurement.

On the Input Sources tab, the "Input source" list lets you select the language you want to type in. You can choose anything from Afghan Dari to Welsh, which can mean a lot of scrolling. To speed things up, use the search box below the list to find the language you are after. You can choose as many languages as you like and switch among them using the flag menu extra that appears in your menu bar automatically when you select multiple languages. So you don't have to spend all day changing languages, you can assign the languages globally or locally, respectively, using the radio buttons labeled "Use the same one in all documents" and "Allow a different one for each document."

Turning on "Show Input menu in menu bar" adds a multicolor flag to the otherwise grayscale menu bar. If you check the box labeled Keyboard & Character Viewer (at the top of the list of input sources), you'll be able to launch the Character Viewer and Keyboard Viewer from the menu bar.

Security & Privacy

The Security & Privacy pane looks like the one included with previous versions of OS X, but Mountain Lion has brought some substantial changes you might miss if you don't scrutinize the pane. The biggest changes are on the General and Privacy tabs. On the General tab, you can invoke Apple's new Gatekeeper technology, and the Privacy tab lets you control which apps know where you are.

Even if these new features of this pane aren't of interest to you, spending a little time in the Security & Privacy preference pane is a wise investment of time. Five minutes in this pane can make you much safer, your data more inaccessible, and your location known only to you. Or, if it is your wish, you can use this pane to leave your Mac completely unprotected. The following sections explain what's on each of the pane's tabs.

General tab

If you want to spend 30 seconds making your Mac much safer, the General tab is the place to visit. The first option on this tab is "Require password ___ after sleep or screen saver begins," which lets you fill in that blank with "immediately" or a duration you select from the pop up menu. This makes it so that anyone who wants to use your computer has to enter a password if the screensaver has started or if your Mac has been asleep. This requires more typing on your part, but it's likely worth the inconvenience, especially if you're using your Mac in a public setting. *Not* requiring a password lets anyone who walks by shake your mouse and start poking around. So unless you log out every time you're away from your Mac for more than 30 seconds, seriously consider enabling this option.

The rest of the options on the General tab are for administrators only. You can click the lock in the pane's lower left and then type in an administrator username and password to make changes to the following settings:

Show a message when the screen is locked

> Turn on this setting and then click the Set Lock Message button and type the message that you want to appear under the login window when your screen is locked.

Disable automatic login

> Checking this box means all users will have to log in each time the computer is restarted.

Below a faint dividing line, you'll discover three more options. You can't tell by looking at them, but these options are part of Mountain Lion's new Gatekeeper security feature designed to help protect your Mac from malware. Gatekeeper lets you specify which applications are allowed to run on your Mac:

Mac App Store

> This option allows your Mac to run only applications you've downloaded directly from the Mac App Store. Since every app in the Mac App Store has been approved by Apple, this is the safest choice, though also the most restrictive. As of March 1, 2012, all apps in the Mac App Store were required to have *sandboxing* enabled. (Sandboxing doesn't mean much to the average user, but it has a big impact on your system. Sandboxed apps can access only the parts of your system that they need access to in order to function, thus limiting the damage they can cause.)

Mac App Store and identified developers

> This option lets you install apps from both the Mac App Store and ones that have been created by developers with Apple-distributed developer IDs. Developers with these credentials digitally sign the applications they create, which allows OS X to check whether or not the app has been altered. If it has, you'll be informed of that fact, and you'll have to manually allow the app to make network connections and the like.

Anywhere
> This option is what you're used to if you've used previous versions of OS X; it lets you install apps from anywhere and made by anyone. While convenient, this option offers the least amount of protection from malware.

If you're familiar with earlier versions of OS X, you'll realize that some of the options that used to be in this pane have apparently disappeared. Turns out the options are still around; you just have to click the Advanced button to see them. When you do so, your reward is a mini pane with the following options:

Log out after __ minutes of activity
> This is a little redundant if you already require a password to wake the computer or to get past the screensaver, but for total control, this is a better option. You can force your Mac to log out after any period of inactivity between 1 and 960 minutes (that's 16 hours!). This option will attempt to shut down any applications you're running, so save your work before you wander away (at least until Auto Save is universally supported).

Require an administrator password to access locked preferences with lock icons
> System Preferences are powerful, so you wouldn't want just anyone mucking with them. Check this box to force users to authenticate themselves before changing any preferences in a pane that has a lock icon in its lower-left corner.

Automatically update safe downloads list
> This setting, which is turned on by default, lets you opt out of Safari's daily update of safe downloads. These updates help protect you against malware such as MacDefender.mpkg. If you download a dangerous file and it is on Apple's list of known malicious software, you'll get a message telling you to move it to the Trash. (The list is stored on your Mac but gets updated every day.) Turn off this setting and you're taking chances you don't want to take.

Disable remote control infrared receiver

By default, unless it's a Mac Pro, your Mac will accept input from almost any infrared device. This can pose a security risk and be very annoying if you're using Apple TV and your laptop. Turn this behavior off by checking the box. If you want to use a remote with your Mac but have it ignore all *other* remotes, click the Pair button and follow the instructions that appear.

FileVault tab

Mountain Lion includes FileVault, which provides an extra layer of security for your data. When enabled, FileVault encrypts your entire drive with XTS-AES 128 encryption, the same algorithm used by governments to protect classified data. You might think all that encrypting and decrypting would burden your system, but OS X manages this trick on the fly so you won't notice a substantial slowdown because of FileVault.

FileVault is turned off by default, but if you decide to enable it by clicking Turn On FileVault, your computer will generate a 24-character recovery key. Committing that key to memory would be a chore, so you can opt to store the key with Apple by clicking the appropriate radio button when the next page pops up. If you do choose to store your key with Apple, it'll be encrypted. Apple will issue the key only if you can answer a security question exactly the way you did when you set up FileVault. (In other words, you won't have to remember the long security key, but you *will* have to remember the answer.) After you make your choice, restart your Mac and your disk will be encrypted.

WARNING

If you forget your login password *and* lose your recovery key, your data is gone forever.

Firewall tab

The Firewall tab relates to your Internet and network connections. The default setting is off, which means your Mac will listen to and respond to just about anything coming over the network: network traffic, pings, and assorted signals that you're never aware of. Surprisingly, this usually isn't a problem if you use your home network or other trusted network all the time. Your router (or the router of other trusted networks) has a firewall built in, so your Mac's firewall would be a bit redundant. But if you're constantly joining iffy WiFi hotspots with your MacBook, you should probably enable the firewall.

To do that, check the lock icon in the pane's lower left and, if it's locked, click it and then type in your administrator name and password. Then simply click the Turn On Firewall button. The dot next to the Firewall status entry will turn green to let you know the firewall is up and running.

Now that the firewall is running, you might be wondering what it's actually *doing*. To find out, click the Firewall Options button. When you do, you'll get some settings that let you tweak how Mountain Lion's firewall performs. The first one is "Block all incoming connections"; if you check this box, Mountain Lion will listen to incoming connections only for very specific, necessary network communications. You'll also see a message appear warning you that turning on this setting prohibits you from using sharing services such as screen sharing and file sharing.

A less inhibiting option is "Automatically allow signed software to receive incoming connections." With this setting turned on (which it is by default when the firewall is enabled), software that's been signed (meaning its author is known to Apple and OS X has confirmed that it hasn't been altered or corrupted) is allowed to receive incoming connections. Every Apple application on your Mac has been signed, so you don't need to worry about killing any of the built-in applications. You can also give applications the green light even if they aren't signed by clicking the + button and adding them to the list of programs that are allowed to communicate.

NOTE

You don't need to try to think of all your unsigned applications and add them to this list. A better tactic is to wait for an application to try to connect to the network; if it's unsigned, OS X will ask if you want to let the program accept incoming connections. Click Accept and that program will be added to this list.

If you check the box next to "Enable stealth mode," your Mac will be less visible on the network. For example, should some nefarious person try to scan all ports at your IP for a way in, they'll get no response; it'll seem like no computer exists at the scanned IP address. However, network activity you engage in —such as visiting a web page or checking email—can reveal your presence on the network.

Privacy

This tab has been completely redone in Mountain Lion. While the old functionality is there, the look is totally different; see Figure 5-2.

On the left side of the pane is a list of services and information that apps can access: Location Services, Contacts, Twitter, Diagnostics & Usage. (If you haven't made your Mac aware of your Twitter existence, Twitter won't appear in the sidebar.)

On the right half of the pane, you'll see what apps can access said information. If you're thinking that it seems like a lot to control manually (who wants to open up System Preferences to allow a Twitter app to access your Twitter account?), don't worry—this pane is simply for *revoking* the ability of apps to access certain information. If an app wants to access your location, for example, a dialog box will pop up so you can grant it access right from that dialog box. So you need to open this pane only to revoke an app's permission to access said data.

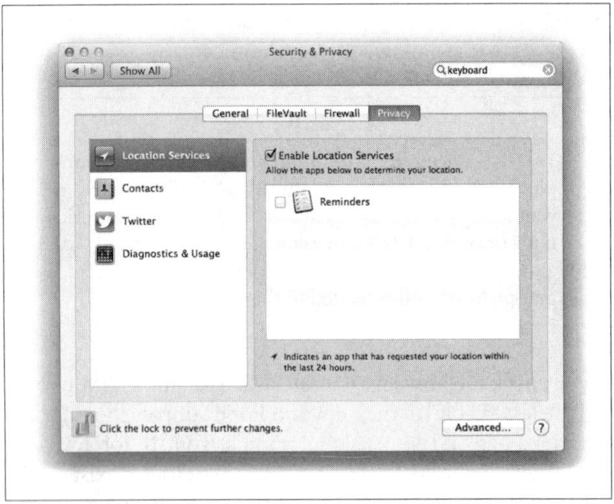

Figure 5-2. The Privacy tab

Spotlight

The Spotlight preference pane has two tabs. The Search Results tab lets you adjust the order of results returned by Spotlight searches (drag items in the list here to change their order in the results) and change the Spotlight menu and window shortcuts. The Privacy tab allows you to exclude folders and disks (but not individual files) from Spotlight's searches. For more on Spotlight, see "Searching with Spotlight" on page 94.

Notifications

Notifications is new to OS X, but it will be familiar if you've been using iOS 5. Notifications provides a centralized location where all your apps can alert you that something is going on. It's a nifty feature: instead of a dozen apps bugging you in a dozen different ways, they can all bother you in the *same* way.

On the left side of the Notifications preference pane is a list of all the apps that will notify you when they have information you need to know. For example, if you're having a text chat and someone sends you a message, you'll be alerted via the Notification Center, a panel that opens on the right side of your screen. How you'll be alerted is up to you (more on that in a moment), but to see all your recent notifications you can either click the Notification Center symbol at the right end of the menu bar or, if you're using a trackpad, swipe with two fingers starting on the right edge of the trackpad and moving left (a two-finger swipe from anywhere else closes the Notification Center panel).

NOTE

If you're wondering whether there's a keyboard shortcut or mouse maneuver that lets you open the Notification Center, the answer is no. Instant access to recent notifications is available only with a trackpad; if you prefer a mouse, you'll have to click the Notification Center symbol.

The Notification Center shows you all your recent notifications, but constantly opening it would be a burden. However, notifications don't have to just show up in the Notification Center; you can also make them appear as banners or alerts by tweaking the settings in the Notifications preference pane. (Banners float in the right corner of your screen and automatically disappear after a few seconds, while alerts require you to acknowledge them with a click; you can also choose None, which leaves the alert visible only in the Notification Center.) The style of notification is determined on an app-by-app basis. Click an app on the left side of the pane, and then choose how you want to be alerted in the right side of the pane.

The Notifications preference pane gives you a few more options, too. The "Show in Notification Center" checkbox controls which apps appear in the Notifications Center. By default, there are nine apps included (they're all listed in the In Notification Center column), and that number will likely grow as you install new apps (apps are automatically added to the Notification Center). Eventually, you'll reach the point where you're getting bothered by too many apps. To banish an app from the Notifications Center, uncheck the "Show in Notification Center" box. It isn't gone forever, though; if you scroll to the bottom of the In Notification Center column, you'll see a Not In Notification Center section. To put the once-banished app back in the Notifications Center, simply click the app in that column and then check the "Show in Notification Center box."

The "Show in Notification Center" setting also lets you control how many messages each app displays in the Notifications Center. The default is five recent items, but you can choose as many as 20 or as few as one instead. You can also adjust the order in which apps appear in the Notification Center by dragging them up or down in the In Notification Center column. So if you want notifications of new email messages to appear at the top of the center, simply drag the Mail item to the top of the column. Or, if you'd prefer that your most recent notification always appear that the top of the center, then set the Sort Notification Center option (it's below the In Notification Center column) to "By time."

The "Badge app icon with notification count" checkbox controls whether apps in the Notifications Center are badged. A badge is a red circle with the number of notifications that appears on the app's icon. The most familiar example of this is likely the Mail icon, which displays the number of unread emails in this fashion. With notifications, this behavior can be redundant, so uncheck this box to make those red badges disappear.

The last setting lets you decide whether you want an audible alert to go with your notifications. If you want the audio reminder, leave the box next to "Play sound when receiving notifications" checked. If you prefer to be notified only visually, uncheck this box.

CDs and DVDs

If your Mac has an optical disk drive, this preference pane controls what your machine does when you insert an optical disk. You can even tell it to do different things depending on the type of disk: a blank CD or DVD, a music CD, a picture CD, or a video DVD. When you click one of the drop-down menus, you'll see Apple's recommended action (the audio CD menu includes Open iTunes, for example), but you aren't limited to just the predefined options. Choosing "Open other application..." will bring up your Applications folder so you can choose any program you like. Or you can opt to have a script run when you insert a disk; if you choose this option, you'll be presented with the familiar window that lets you browse to where the script you want to use is saved.

Displays

If you own a laptop or an iMac, you probably won't visit this preference pane until you need to connect a second monitor or projector. On the other hand, if you're a color perfectionist or need to connect your Mac to a non-Apple display, stopping by the Displays pane is necessary. This is where you control your monitor's resolution, color depth, brightness, and color to fit your needs. (Depending on what kind of monitor you're using, you might see a tab labeled Options with settings related to the specific monitor you're using.)

If you're using multiple monitors, clicking Arrangement allows you to set the location of the menu bar, enable display mirroring, and configure the spatial arrangement of each screen so it corresponds to how the displays are physically arranged.

This is also where you'd *expect* to find an option to run two or more applications in Full Screen mode. Sadly, that's not an option: even if you have 10 monitors attached to your Mac, when you use a full-screen app, the other monitors will change to a gray linen pattern and convey no useful information.

Energy Saver

You get different options in this preference pane depending on what kind of Mac you're using. On a MacBook, you'll see two tabs—Battery and Power Adapter—which makes sense because you'll likely want different settings when you're using the power adapter than when you're relying on the battery. Also, the "Show battery status in the menu bar" checkbox is turned on by default, giving you a quick way to see how much power you have left. (If you feel that the menu bar on your Mac is too crowded, unchecking this box will free up a tiny bit of space.)

The options on both laptops and desktops are very similar. The slider next to "Computer sleep" controls the delay between the time you stop using your Mac and the time it enters sleep mode, a low-power mode that uses much less power than when it's "awake." Although Mountain Lion will restart all your apps when you restart your machine, waking it from sleep is a much faster process. The "Display sleep" slider adjusts how long it takes for your screen to turn off to save power. (The two tabs on a laptop—Battery and Power Adapter—let you to set different values for when your Mac and display go to sleep depending on the current power source.)

Under the sliders are some checkboxes (they vary slightly between the Battery and Power Adapter tabs):

Wake for network access
> If you use Back to My Mac or have a copy of Apple Remote Desktop, you'll probably want to leave this box checked; it allows your Mac to wake up when you want to log in remotely.

Slightly dim the display when using this power source (laptops only)
> This option is on the Battery tab. As you can probably guess, it's supposed to extend battery life by making the display use less energy when you're relying on battery

power. In practice, most people don't notice the difference in battery life.

Start up automatically after a power failure

Checking this box means that if the power flickers, your Mac will start up again as soon as the power comes back on. Your Mac doesn't really know that the power has gone out; it just knows that shutdown protocol wasn't followed. If you accidentally hit the off button on a surge protector, your Mac will start up when the button is moved back to the on position, too. (For obvious reasons, this option isn't available on MacBooks' Battery tab.)

If you're a very consistent person, you can get the best of all worlds by clicking the Schedule button. This brings up a pane where you can tell your Mac when to start up or wake, and when to shut down, sleep, or restart by choosing a schedule from the pop-up menus and entering times in the boxes. For example, if you're sitting in front of your Mac every weekday by 8:07, then having your machine automatically start up at 8:03 can save you a few minutes of waiting each day.

Keyboard

The Keyboard preference pane is where you can change key commands (see Chapter 8 for a list of common ones) and how your keyboard responds to typing. The pane is divided into two tabs—Keyboard and Keyboard Shortcuts—and includes a Set Up Bluetooth Keyboard button. If you've got a Bluetooth keyboard that your computer hasn't recognized automatically, then click this button to make OS X attempt to pair with it.

Keyboard tab

This tab has two sliders: the Key Repeat slider lets you adjust how frequently a key will register if you hold it down, and the Delay Until Repeat slider controls how long you have to hold a key down before your Mac starts registering that key repeatedly. The Keyboard tab also gives you the option to use all the numbered F keys as standard function keys. If you turn on this option, those keys won't work the same as before; for example, pressing F10 won't mute your Mac, it'll invoke Exposé instead (to mute your Mac, you'll need to press the Fn *and* F10 keys at the same time).

Turning on the "Show Keyboard & Character Viewers in menu bar" checkbox creates a menu extra that gives you easy access to characters (arrows and such) with the Character Viewer and the Keyboard Viewer's simulated keyboard that shows what the modifier keys do when pressed.

NOTE

If you're using a laptop, you get a few more settings to play with: a checkbox labeled "Adjust keyboard brightness in low light" and a slider labeled "Turn off when computer is not used for"; the slider includes durations that range from "5 secs" to Never.

Click Input Sources to see the "Input source" list, which lets you type in different languages; simply select the language you want to type in from the list on the left. To save you some scrolling, use the search box at the bottom of the window to find the language you're after. You can choose as many languages as you like and switch among them at will using the flag menu extra that appears in the menu bar automatically when you select multiple languages. So that you don't have to spend all day changing languages, you can choose to assign the languages globally or locally using the radio buttons labeled "Use the same one in all documents" and "Allow a different one for each document," respectively.

Keyboard Shortcuts tab

This is where you can adjust the key commands used by your Mac. On the left side of the pane is a list of applications and features so you can locate the ones you want to change. To change a key command, double-click it in the list on the right and then press the key(s) you want to use instead. You can use

the function keys or keys with modifiers as your new choice.
Figure 5-3 shows an example.

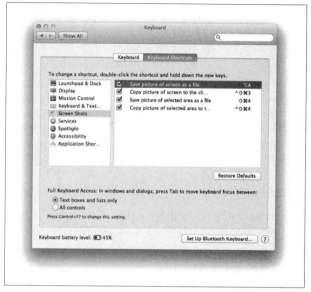

Figure 5-3. Changing the key command for screenshots

To add a *new* key command, select Application Shortcuts in
the left column, and then click the + button. You'll see a pop-
up menu of applications you can add keyboard commands to.
Select an application, type the *exact* name of the menu command you want to create a keyboard shortcut for into the Menu
Title box, and then type the key(s) you want to use as the
shortcut. For example, there's no keyboard command for customizing the toolbar in the Finder. To create one, select Finder
from the pop-up menu, type **Customize Toolbar...** (*with* the
dots) into the Menu Title box, and then click the Keyboard
Shortcut field and type your shortcut. After that, when a Finder
window is active, you can hit that key and the Customize Toolbar window will show up. As a bonus, the key command you
added will also appear next to the command's name in the

Finder's View menu. If you tire of your custom key command, open the Keyboard preference pane, click the shortcut once, and then hit the – key; your key command will be banished from the preference pane *and* from the application. The Restore Defaults button below the list of keyboard shortcuts will also ax your custom key command and any other changes you've made.

Below the two lists, this tab also includes a setting for Full Keyboard Access (a way for you to interact with your Mac without using the mouse). If you switch this setting from the default "Text boxes and lists only" to "All controls," you'll be able to use the Tab key to move from field to field in most applications.

Mouse

Plan on using a mouse with your Mac? This preference pane lets you set up a Bluetooth mouse and customize your mousing options.

NOTE

If you used Lion, you probably either loved or hated its default scrolling behavior, which was called "Scroll direction: natural" and mirrored the way you scroll on an iPad or iPhone. Apparently, a lot of people were in the "do not want" camp when it came to this setting. In Mountain Lion, the default is the way you're used to if you've been using anything besides Lion. To get "natural" scroll direction back, you'll have to visit the Mouse or Trackpad preference pane.

Magic Mouse options

If you've got a Magic Mouse, the Point & Click tab of this preference pane allows you to turn "Scroll direction: natural" on or off, decide whether you want a secondary click (known as a "right-click" to everyone but Apple) with your Magic

Mouse and how you want said click enacted, and turn smart zooming off or on. You also get a mouse battery–level indicator and a slider for adjusting tracking (how fast the mouse pointer moves on screen in response to physical mouse movements).

On the More Gestures tab, you can turn on "Swipe between pages," "Swipe between full-screen apps," and an option to launch Mission Control with a double-tap. Each gesture comes with a nifty movie explaining how to pull off the necessary taps and swipes. To watch the movie, put your cursor over the gesture you're interested in and the instructional video will play automatically.

Mighty Mouse options

If you're using a Mighty Mouse, you'll find sliders for adjusting tracking, double-clicking, and scrolling speeds. You'll also see pop-up menus for every part of the Mighty Mouse that can detect pushes. Each menu lets you specify what happens when you press that button. You can choose from a multitude of actions to assign to each button, including secondary clicks and application launching.

After you're done setting up the buttons, you can control how the Mighty Mouse scrolls by choosing from the pop-up menu next to Scrolling. You can turn it off, have it scroll vertically only, scroll vertically and horizontally, or scroll 360 degrees.

You can also set up your Mighty Mouse to zoom by checking the box next to Zoom. You get to select the modifier key that will invoke zooming when you're using the scroll ball. If you click the Options button, you'll find some settings that let you fine-tune its scrolling behavior.

If you're using a non-Apple mouse

Some people don't like Apple's mice, and that's OK—your Mac will happily work with non-Apple mice. Some mice ship with custom drivers, but most can work with your Mac straight out of the box. The customization options you see in the Mouse preference pane depend on the model you're using.

Trackpad

Your options here depend on which MacBook model you have. On newer MacBooks with multitouch trackpads (which were introduced on the MacBook Air in 2008), you'll get the options described in the multitouch section below and shown in Figure 5-4. (You'll get that same set of options if you're using Apple's Magic Trackpad.) If you have an older MacBook, you'll get a different set of options, though some of the settings are the same as on multitouch machines.

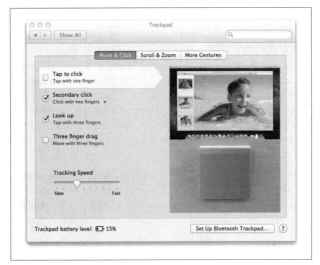

Figure 5-4. The preferences for a multitouch trackpad

Multitouch trackpads

In the Trackpad preference pane, you can adjust your Mac-Book's tracking speed, set up a Bluetooth trackpad, and configure gestures. On the "Point and Click" tab, you can enable "Tap to click" (which makes your Mac interpret a light tap as a click), "Secondary click" (a.k.a. "right-clicking"), "Look up" (a feature that looks up words with OS X's built-in Dictionary), and three-finger dragging.

When you click the Scroll & Zoom tab, you'll find the following options: "Scroll direction: natural," "Zoom in or out," "Smart zoom," and "Rotate."

The More Gestures tab includes six different options. You can turn on "Swipe between pages" and tell your Mac how you want to gesture to invoke that function. You can do the same with "Swipe between full-screen apps," Mission Control, and App Exposé. Launchpad and "Show Desktop gestures" aren't customizable; you can only turn them on or off.

As with the Magic Mouse, these gestures aren't always self-explanatory, so each gesture comes with a little movie showing you how to pull it off. Put your cursor over the option you want explained and the associated movie will automatically start playing. (One supposes it has been a good time for hand models in the Cupertino area.)

Print & Scan

This preference pane is, unsurprisingly, where you add and remove printers and scanners. To add a device, click the tiny + button on the left side of the pane, and Mountain Lion will look for nearby printers and scanners and set them up for you. To remove a printer or scanner, select it in the list and then click the – button beneath the list. The rest of the options you see in this pane depend on the exact model of printer or scanner you have installed.

Sound

The Sound preference pane is divided into three tabs: Sound Effects, Output, and Input. The "Output volume" slider is always visible at the bottom of the pane, regardless of which tab you're on. There's a checkbox below that slider that lets you get rid of the Volume menu extra. If you're wondering how you'll control the volume with the menu extra gone, remember that you can use the keyboard for that trick: use the F10–F12 keys on Apple keyboards.

Sound Effects tab

The Sound Effects tab allows you to choose an alert sound. To preview a sound, click it in the list or use the arrows to move up and down. Mountain Lion gives you plenty of options for audio alerts, so hopefully you can find something to your liking.

The next question is where you want the alert sounds to come from. If you have speakers plugged into your Mac, you can opt to send the sound either through them or through the computer's built-in speaker(s).

Below that is a slider for adjusting the alert volume if, for example, you want alert sounds to be softer than the rest of the sounds coming out of your Mac (you don't want Basso walking all over iTunes, right?). Note that the maximum alert volume is the same as the master volume for your system, so if you want alerts to be the loudest noise coming out of your Mac, you're out of luck unless you can turn down the volume of other sound-generating programs.

Finally, you get two or three checkboxes so you hear the sounds you want and skip the ones you don't. By checking the box next to each entry, you can do the following:

- Play or silence user interface sounds (such as the noise the Trash makes when being emptied).
- Play feedback when volume is changed (with this turned on, if you hit a volume key or move the volume slider, the alert sound will play at the new volume).

Output tab

The Sound Effects tab lets you decide which speakers play alert sounds; the Output tab lets you decide where everything *else* is played. For example, you can choose between your Mac Pro's internal speaker (not great for an immersive media experience) or the top-of-the-line speakers you plugged into the optical out port. Headphones are a special case, as plugging in headphones mutes the internal speakers.

You also might see some extra options depending on your hardware. For example, if you're using the built-in speakers on an iMac or MacBook, you get to adjust the left-right balance with a slider.

Input tab

This tab is where you control your Mac's "ears." If you're using anything other than a Mac Mini or a Mac Pro, your computer has a built-in internal microphone, which is the default selection for sound input. This means that any audio chats, video chats, or podcasts you record will get recorded via that internal mic. If you want to use a USB microphone instead, plug it in and select it from the list on this tab.

Another option on this tab is "Input volume," which controls how "hot" (as they say in the radio business) the sound coming into your Mac will be. Turn it all the way up and anyone you're chatting with will reach for his or her volume controls a millisecond into the conversation.

Turning on "Use ambient noise reduction" tells your Mac to ignore the sounds going on around you—screaming kids, howling wolves, or what have you. It isn't perfect, but it helps when you're chatting or, more importantly, using voice commands with your Mac.

iCloud

iCloud is the system OS X uses to keep your Mac synced with your iPhone, your iPad, and any other Macs you own. The iCloud preference pane is where you control what stuff you want synced up and how much iCloud storage space you're using.

This preference pane is, in true Apple fashion, extremely simple. There's a list of apps with checkboxes beside them. Checking a box means data for that app will be shared with any other devices logged in to your iCloud account. (The sections below explain how iCloud relates to each app in the list.)

NOTE

If you click the Sign Out button in the iCloud preference pane, you'll be hit with fifty questions. The rub is that signing out of iCloud will delete your iCloud contacts from your Mac, turn off your Photo Stream, delete iCloud calendars from your Mac, and so forth. You can choose to keep local copies on your Mac, but it's easiest to just remain logged in.

At the bottom of the pane is a green bar that indicates how much of the iCloud disk space allotted to you is being used (Figure 5-5). If you're bumping up against your limit, you might want to spend some time managing your data. To do so, click Manage to bring up a list that shows just what is using your space and how much space it's using.

Figure 5-5. Preparing to delete some Doodle Jump data.

For most of the items in the list, you can simply select the app, backup, or document, single-click the data you want to delete, and then hit the Delete key to erase the memory-hogging data. The exception is Mail: if your email is using up too much space, you have to take a trip to the Mail app and delete any extraneous messages and folders there.

Contacts

When you're using iCloud, any changes you make to your contacts (adding, deleting, or modifying them) on one device are automatically reflected on all your other devices. It's a convenient feature (and one that you're likely already used to).

Calendar & Reminders

The Calendar app on your Mac takes care of all your calendaring chores, but you're not always in front of your Mac when you want to make an appointment or change a meeting time. With iCloud, changes you make on one device are pushed to (automatically shared with) all your devices. And as you likely expect, you can also create calendars that others can subscribe to and update. If you're running a Cub Scout den, for example, all the members can update the calendar as needed, and the changes will be pushed to everyone subscribed to that calendar.

Reminders work the same way: create a reminder on your iPhone, and it will show up on your Mac, and vice versa.

Notes

Check this box and any entry you make in the Notes app will show up on all your iCloud-enabled devices.

Safari

In Lion, this option was labeled Bookmarks, but it has been improved in Mountain Lion. If you check this box, then not only will your bookmarks be synchronized across your devices, but the pages and tabs you currently have open will be, too. So if you're browsing your favorite site on your Mac and then decide to pick up your iPad, then the same site will be open on the tablet when you launch Safari there.

Photo Stream

One of the niftier and, with the advent of iOS 5, most necessary features of iCloud is Photo Stream. When you upload pictures to your Mac, or snap a photo (or record a video) with your iPhone, the photo (or video) gets published to your Photo Stream for you to see on all your devices. Apple stores a copy of your last 1,000 photos for the last 30 days so you'll have plenty of time to drag the photo into a library to save it on your Mac forever.

To enable Photo Stream, make sure you're signed in to iCloud and then open iPhoto '11; you'll be greeted by a splash page asking you if you want to enable Photo Stream. To turn Photo Stream off on your Mac while leaving it on for other devices, head to iPhoto→File→Preferences, and then click on the Photo Stream icon. To turn it off for all your devices, uncheck the Photo Stream checkbox in this preference pane.

NOTE

Happily, any photos and videos in your Photo Stream don't count against your free 5 GB of iCloud storage.

Documents & Data

You've probably been in a position where you have a document on your PC at work and would like to tweak that document on your Mac or iOS device. If you have iWork iOS apps (Keynote, Pages, or Numbers) on your iOS devices, you're in luck. To make documents from your Mac or PC available anywhere, head to *www.icloud.com/iwork*, log in with your Apple ID and password, and then simply drag and drop any documents you'd like to share. To edit those documents on your Mac (or PC), log into that same site and you'll be able to modify the documents in your browser.

NOTE

While iCloud will happily work with Microsoft Office documents, you won't be able to do anything with them until you have one of the iWork iOS apps installed on at least one of your iOS devices.

Unlike photos, documents (the ones you add to iCloud) and data (your contacts and so forth) *do* count against your 5 GB storage limit.

Back to My Mac

This feature allows you to access your Mac from any other computer—useful if you've left that really important file at home and you're giving a presentation in Toledo. Just hop on the hotel's computer and you'll be able to get that Keynote presentation everyone is dying to see.

NOTE

How well Back to My Mac works depends on how your router is configured. If your Mac doesn't like your router's configuration, it will tell you what you need to do to get maximum performance.

Find My Mac

Do you suffer from the horrors of a misplaced Mac? It can be unnerving when you wonder whether you left your MacBook Air on a park bench or in your room. Fortunately, you can find that lost Mac.

Find My Mac offers a bit more than just the ability to find your Mac. You can also remotely make your Mac play a sound (in case you left it under a couch cushion) or you can send a message to it (like "OMG reward for return!!!!"). If those measures aren't enough, you can also lock your Mac remotely, preventing anyone from accessing your Mac unless they enter the correct four-digit code. You also have a nuclear option, Remote Wipe, which deletes all the data on your Mac. This is great for keeping your info safe but, should you later locate your Mac, you'll have to restore all your data (though that's not a big deal if you've been using Time Machine regularly).

You can find your stray Mac by heading to *www.iCloud.com*, logging in, and clicking Find My iPhone. When you do, all the devices you have registered with iCloud will show up. Click the device you're interested in and you'll get a good idea of where it is (Figure 5-6). If you want your Mac to do something, click the blue "i" and then tell your Mac what to do. (If you have only one device registered, you'll be able to skip the blue "i" step and just tell your Mac to play a sound or send a message.)

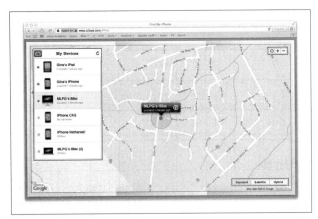

Figure 5-6. Looks like my iMac is at home

Mail, Contacts & Calendars

Instead of setting up mail accounts in Mail, juggling calendars in iCal, and so on, this pane lets you set up your accounts once in a centralized location. Messages, Mail, Address Book, and other apps use the information you enter here to keep you current.

When you first open this pane, it will look on your Mac for email and chat accounts and automatically add them. If you're setting up a new Mac, this pane comes with iCloud, Microsoft Exchange, Gmail, Yahoo!, Twitter, Flickr, Vimeo, and AOL accounts preconfigured, so if you're using one of those (and you probably are), just click it in the list. When you do, a window will pop up asking for your name, email address, and password. Once you've supplied your credentials, you're allowed to check the services you want to use from that provider (mail, calendars and reminders, Messages and notes).

If your service isn't listed, click Add Other Account (at the bottom of the list) and get ready to do a little bit of work. The prelisted services all provide calendars, chat, contact, and mail accounts; to get the same functions from another service, you'll have to set these up individually.

Network

You can guess what this preference pane does: it controls your network configuration. At the top of the pane is the Location menu. By default, it's set to Automatic, but if you use your Mac in more than one place, you might want to add a location. To do so, pick Edit Locations from this menu; in the window that appears, click the + sign and then add your location.

On the left side of the Network pane, you'll see all the ways your Mac can connect to the network (typically WiFi, Ethernet, and FireWire, but this can vary according to the model of your Mac). If a network is connected, it'll have a green light next to it (unconnected networks have red lights). It's possible to have more than one active network connection—a WiFi connection and an Ethernet connection, perhaps. If that's the case, you can drag the connections around in the list to match your preferred order of connecting. For example, dragging Ethernet to the top will force your Mac to use the Ethernet connection before the WiFi connection.

To the right of the list of networks, you'll find information about and options for your current network. This is where you can find your IP address and settings related to the kind of connection you're using (like a Turn Wi-Fi Off button, for example). For wired networks, you get to pick how you want to configure IPv4 (you can get this information from your ISP, but most use DCHP, and your Mac will be able to take care of this for you). You'll also see an Advanced button that you can click to bring up six different tabs. Configuring these tabs usually isn't necessary and is beyond the scope of this book.

The best thing about the Network preference pane is the "Assist me" button at the bottom of it. If you're having problems setting up your network, clicking this button and following the directions will likely solve them. The Revert button, as you can guess, will undo any changes you've made to your network settings, and Apply tells the preference pane to implement your changes.

Bluetooth

Predictably, this is the go-to panel if you're using a Bluetooth device or if you want to display a Bluetooth status icon in your menu bar. This panel includes a list of all the discoverable Bluetooth devices nearby (in other words, ones your Mac can connect to) and their current connection statuses. If you click the Sharing Setup button, you'll open the Sharing preference pane (described next). If you click the Advanced button, you'll get the following options:

- Open Bluetooth Setup Assistant at startup if no keyboard is detected
- Open Bluetooth Setup Assistant at startup if no mouse or trackpad is detected
- Allow Bluetooth devices to wake this computer
- Reject incoming audio requests

The descriptions below each option explain what they're for. You'll also find an area that lists (and allows you to adjust) Bluetooth devices that use serial ports on your Mac.

Sharing

This preference pane allows you to share a variety of files and bits of hardware over your network (all of these options are off by default):

DVD or CD Sharing
> This option lets other computers use the optical drive in your Mac. There's also a checkbox to have your Mac ask you before anyone accesses its optical drive.

Screen Sharing
> Allows other computers to view your screen and control your computer over the network. You can specify which users are allowed to connect or allow all users. If you'd like to let people connect from non-Mac computers, click Computer Settings and then enable the VNC (Virtual Network Computing) option; they'll need a VNC client such as RealVNC or TightVNC for this to work.

File Sharing
> File sharing allows others to access your shared files over the network, which is a nifty way to trade files. If you turn this option on, make sure you create a strong password.

> With file sharing turned on, users on other computers have a few ways to connect to your machine. If those users are on the same local network, they can get to your computer by heading to the Finder's menu bar and choosing Go→Connect to Server. The address they'll need to access your computer is your Mac's name with *.local* appended.

> It may be even easier than that, though. OS X features a zero-configuration networking protocol called Bonjour. Folks who have Bonjour will see other computers that they can access in the sidebar of their Finder windows.

Either way, users will have to supply a username and password to connect. (You may want to set up a sharing-only user for this—see "User Accounts" on page 33).

If you want to access your files from another Mac while away from your home or work network, you can use Back to My Mac (see "Back to My Mac" on page 151).

Printer Sharing

Checking this box turns your Mac into a print server. That means that, if you're on a laptop and want to print something in the basement, say, you won't have to haul your carcass over to the printer or even send the file to the Mac connected to the printer for later printing. Just check the Printer Sharing box on the Mac that's hooked up to the printer and you can print from anywhere on your local area network.

Scanner Sharing

This is Printer Sharing's less-used little brother, and it works in much the same way: if you've got a scanner connected to the host Mac, you can use it from a remote computer.

Remote Login

This lets users connect to your Mac over SSH (secure shell). To do that, they'll need to open a Terminal window (Applications→Utilities→Terminal) and either use the *ssh* command-line utility or select Shell→New Remote Connection.

Remote Management

If you have a copy of Apple Remote Desktop and want to use it to connect to your Mac, make sure this box is checked. (Remote Management is a lot like screen sharing except that it's designed for people controlling more than one Mac at a time, as you might find in a classroom setting.)

Remote Apple Events

Checking this box will let other Macs send Apple Events to your computer. What are Apple Events? They are wide ranging, but just about anything AppleScript can do can be an Apple Event.

Internet Sharing

This setting lets you share your Internet connection with other computers. You can choose to share a wired connection via AirPort or share an AirPort connection with another computer wired to yours. If you're doing the former, you can choose to add some security measures.

Bluetooth Sharing

Checking this box allows Bluetooth devices to interact with your Mac. The options here let you customize your Mac's behavior when receiving files, designate a folder for the files your Mac accepts over Bluetooth, set browsing behavior, and designate which folders users can browse on your Mac.

Users and Groups

You can use this preference pane to manage the accounts on your Mac—if you're an administrator, that is. To add or delete accounts, use the + and – buttons under the list of users. (For a complete discussion of managing accounts, see "User Accounts" on page 33.)

Clicking Login Options at the bottom of the list of users lets you enable or disable automatic login and choose what appears in the login window: the "Name and password" setting is more secure than "List of users" because it means that anyone trying to get into your Mac will need to guess both a username *and* password. You also get to decide whether to include Restart, Sleep, and Shut Down buttons in the login window; include the Input menu in the login window; show password hints; and allow use of VoiceOver in the login window.

Finally, you can enable fast user switching, which—as its name implies—lets you switch between accounts without logging out first. You'll still need a password to get back to your account, but if an application was running when you switched users, it'll be running when you come back to your account.

The drop-down menu next to this setting lets you view users by full name, short name, or icon. For more on fast user switching, see "Logging In" on page 42.

Fast user switching is nifty, but you might be wondering if you aren't better off instead using the Resume feature, which restarts everything automatically when you log back in. While the end result is the same, fast user switching is actually a little faster than Resume because the applications aren't fully shut down when you use fast user switching.

Parental Controls

Parental Controls are OS X's way of protecting your kids while they're on the Internet. This preference pane takes some of the worry out of allowing a child to use the Internet unsupervised by letting you set up a variety of rules and filters that control not only which sites they can visit but also what programs they can use and even who they can chat and email with.

NOTE

While Parental Controls are designed for parents whose kids use their computers, you can use them to manage any user who isn't an administrator.

If you haven't set up any additional accounts on your machine (meaning that the only account is your Administrator account), then when you first open this pane, you'll see a message telling you "There are no user accounts to manage." You can then choose to create a new user account with parental controls or convert the account you're currently logged into as one with parental controls. If you pick the former, when you click Continue, you'll see boxes you can fill in to create a new user. If you pick the latter, you'll be asked to create a new Administrator account to replace the user you're currently logged in as. Either way, once you're done filling in the name and password fields, click Continue.

If you do have additional accounts on your Mac, you'll see a list of users on the left side of this pane. Select a user and then click the Enable Parental Controls button to start setting them up. You'll also find an option to "Manage parental controls from another computer" that allows you to manage the controls from afar (you wouldn't want to invade your kids' space, now would you?).

Either way, you'll end up with a list of users on the left of the pane and a set of five tabs on the right. Here's what each of those tabs lets you control.

Apps

This tab allows you to enable a simplified Finder and control which applications the user can run. If you're enabling content controls, controlling which applications the managed user can run is essential.

To give particular applications the green light, click the box next to Limit Applications and then use the settings underneath it to choose applications. Turn off the "Allow User to Modify the Dock" checkbox to revoke that privilege. Clicking the Logs button reveals where your kid has been going, shows where she's tried to go, and gives you access to her Messages transcripts. See something you don't like? Hit the Block button at the bottom of the window to add the website or chat participant to the list of blocked sites or individuals.

Web

This tab is concerned with where people can go while they're on the Internet. It offers three levels of control:

Allow unrestricted access to websites
> Clicking this radio button allows this user complete access to the Web.

Try to limit access to adult websites automatically
> If you click this button, OS X will rely on filters and lists of adult websites and try to block them. It's surprisingly accurate. The downside is that the filters also block all

https (secure) websites, so if your teen is doing online banking, she won't be able to access her account. To allow a particular site or specifically exclude a site that isn't caught by the filter, click the Customize button.

Allow access to only these websites

This is the most restrictive option. The user can visit only the sites listed here, which have all been preapproved by Apple. To add or delete sites, use the + and – buttons below the list.

People

The top part of this tab is brand-new and deals with interactions in the Game Center. The top checkbox allows your child to join multiplayer games, and the lower checkbox allows your child to add Game Center friends. Uncheck either of these boxes if you think this would be a security risk.

This section of the tab limits who the managed user can interact with via Mail, Messages, or both. Once you've checked the appropriate box(es), you have to approve any person who wants to email or chat with your kids by clicking the + button and then typing in the person's email address and instant messaging information.

Time Limits

This tab lets you set a maximum amount of time the computer can be used per day and when. Just drag the sliders to set the durations for weekdays and weekends. Use the Bedtime section to restrict when the user can be on the computer.

Other

This tab includes five options that let you do the following: disable use of dictation (hey, they might be taking a typing class), hide profanity in OS X's built-in dictionaries, prevent the user from printing documents, keep the user from burning CDs and DVDs, and prevent the user from changing the password to his or her account.

Date & Time

The Date & Time tab of this preference pane is where you can set the date using the calendar interface (or by typing it in) and set the time. The "Set date and time automatically" checkbox (which is turned on by default) tells your Mac to fetch the current date and time from the server that's selected in the menu to the right. You can modify your date and time formats by clicking the Open Language & Text button; see "Language & Text" on page 126 for details.

The Time Zone tab, not surprisingly, controls the time zone your Mac uses. There's a checkbox that you can turn on to tell your Mac to pick a zone automatically, but if it guesses wrong, you can set it manually by clicking on the map or providing the name of a major city in your time zone.

The Clock tab gives you the option of showing the current date and time in the menu bar, allows you to choose how the time is displayed there, and lets you tweak a few other options. You can also have your Mac announce the time every hour, half hour, or 15 minutes. Click the Customize Voice button, and you'll be able to change the voice used to announce the time, how loud it is, and even how quickly it speaks.

Software Update

This preference pane is focused on getting updates to OS X and other software from the App Store. (Note that Software Update updates only Apple software and software you've acquired from the App Store.) If you keep the box next to to "Automatically check for updates" turned on, you'll have options to "Download newly available updates in the background" and "Install system data files and security updates." It'll make your life easier to check all these boxes, but if you want to be the undisputed master of your Mac, you can uncheck the boxes and do it all manually by choosing Software Update in the menu.

You also get to decide if you want purchases you made from the App Store to automatically show up on the Mac you're currently using. This is all about convenience. Check the box and the apps you buy elsewhere will automatically show up on the Mac you're using. Leave it unchecked, and when you want to use an app you purchased on another machine, you'll have to go to the App Store to get it (happily, you won't be charged again).

Dictation & Speech

Before Mountain Lion, if you wanted your Mac to take dictation, you needed a third-party program. Now, dictation capabilities come built into OS X, and this is the preference pane for managing your dictation (and speech) needs. It has two tabs:

Dictation tab

This tab lets you select which microphone you want to use by clicking the drop-down menu under the microphone picture. Note that the microphone image changes according to the level of noise detected by your chosen microphone—when there's more noise, more of the microphone image lights up.

To enable Mountain Lion's dictation feature, click the On radio button next to Dictation. Clicking the Shortcut pop-up menu allows you to change the shortcut key to tell your Mac to start taking dictation. Click the Language pop-up menu to pick which language you want to dictate in.

The "About Dictation and Privacy..." button brings up a pane that tells you what Apple uses to help your Mac accurately transcribe your words and how you can restrict access to dictation.

Text to Speech tab

Here's where you control what voice your Mac speaks with. The System Voice menu offers six standard voices, but you can access many more if you choose Customize.... You'll also see a slider to control how fast the voices read selected text. Adjust the slider and then listen to the result by clicking the Play button.

You'll also find three checkboxes that allow you to control when your Mac notifies you audibly. You can have your Mac announce when alerts are displayed (see "Notifications" on page 134). Want more control over the audible alerts? The Set Alert Options button becomes clickable once you check the Announce box; click the button to choose the voice for alerts, pick what phrase your Mac uses (you can even type in your own phrase), and set a delay between when the alert appears and when you're notified (Figure 5-7). The Play button lets you check your settings.

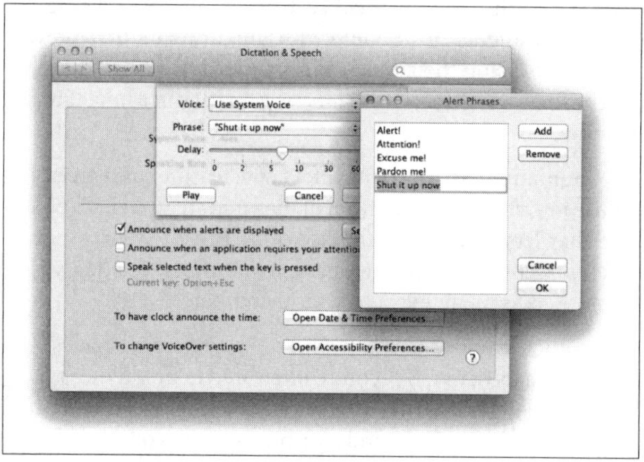

Figure 5-7. Creating a customized alert

You'll also find a checkbox that will make your Mac announce when an app needs attention (this is usually indicated by the app icon jumping up and down in the Dock). The final checkbox gives you the option to have your Mac speak text at a keypress. Check the box and then, if you wish, click the Change

Key button to change the default keyboard shortcut (Option-Esc).

The last two buttons on this tab take you to other preference panes that now handle functions that were controlled by the Speech preference pane in earlier versions of OS X.

Time Machine

Time Machine is Apple's solution to the annoyance of making backups. In this preference pane, you can choose where, what, and when to back up. For more information, see "Time Machine" on page 206.

Accessibility

Until Lion, this pane was called Universal Access. These settings are designed for people with impairments that prevent them from using their Macs in a standard manner—but they can be fun for *anyone* who wants to use a Mac in a nonstandard manner.

In Mountain Lion, this pane offers new features and an easier-to-use interface. At the bottom of the pane are two checkboxes: one that lets you enable the use of assistive devices (such as touchscreens and pointing devices) and one that adds a Universal Access menu extra to your menu bar.

In the middle of this pane, as with other preference panes, you select the aspect of OS X you're interested in modifying via the list on the left (where they're grouped into Seeing, Hearing, and Interacting categories), and the preferences you can change appear on the right side of the pane. The following sections explain what each group of settings lets you adjust.

Display

The Display settings include two checkboxes. The "Invert colors" box does just what you'd expect: displays the opposite color of what your Mac normally would. When this setting is turned on, everything from your desktop image to your Dock icons is displayed in the opposite colors—black turns white, green turns purple, etc. If you want to eschew color altogether, check the "Use grayscale" box (a great way to simulate a retro computing experience).

The Enhance Contrast slider bumps up your monitor's contrast, making subtle details harder to see but text easier to read. The Cursor Size slider controls, well, the size of your cursor.

VoiceOver

VoiceOver is OS X's screen-reading utility, but that simple description doesn't really explain how much you can do with VoiceOver. Since VoiceOver can do so much, these settings include a button labeled Open VoiceOver Training. Clicking that button opens a comprehensive tutorial on how to use VoiceOver that even includes a practice mode. Clicking Open VoiceOver Utility instead lets you control various aspects of VoiceOver. As you might imagine, if you use VoiceOver, you may end up creating a vast number of custom rules and shortcuts, so you'll be pleased to learn about the Portable Preferences feature (which you access by clicking Open VoiceOver Utility). If you're going to use a different Mac, you can take all of your custom settings with you. Simply pop in an external drive (flash drive, etc.), and you'll be able to save your settings and take them along.

Zoom

These settings give you two ways to magnify what's on your screen. You can check the box labeled "Use keyboard shortcuts to zoom" and then use the listed shortcuts. Or you can check the box next to "Use scroll gesture with modifier keys to zoom" and then choose which button you want to press when you want to magnify the screen. For example, if you choose the Control key, then when you press Control while swiping up on your trackpad, the screen will be magnified (the more you swipe, the bigger everything gets). The keyboard shortcuts and scroll gesture options are independent of each other, so if you like you can use *both* methods to zoom.

You'll also find a Smooth Images option. Checking this box will keep text and pictures smooth when you zoom the screen; unchecking it will result in jagged edges.

You also have an option to make zooming follow your *keyboard focus* (the place where the text would show up if you started typing). Keyboard focus is determined by VoiceOver, and if you turn on this setting, the area where your typing is going to appear will be magnified. If you leave this setting off, your Mac will instead zoom based on where your cursor is.

The Zoom Style pop-up menu lets you choose between Full-screen (where everything gets bigger when you zoom) and Picture-in-Picture (where a window will pop up and follow your cursor; only the part of the screen inside that window will be enlarged).

Clicking More Options brings up some ways to fine-tune your zooming experience. You'll find sliders labeled Maximum and Minimum Zoom, a checkbox for showing a preview rectangle when the screen isn't zoomed, and radio buttons for controlling how the screen image moves when you're zoomed in.

Audio

These settings let you make your Mac's screen flash when there's an alert instead of using audio alerts (quite useful when your Mac is muted), and there's an option to play stereo audio in mono.

Mouse & Trackpad

This section allows you to set your double-click speed using a slider, and gives you a box to check if you want your Mac to ignore its built-in trackpad when you're using a different method of controlling the cursor, like a USB mouse or a wireless mouse.

You'll also find two buttons for fine-tuning your trackpad or mouse experience. Clicking Trackpad Options gives you a chance to set the scrolling speed and to enable or disable scrolling with inertia via a pop up menu. If you leave scrolling with inertia enabled, then when you flick the trackpad, whatever window you're viewing will continue to scroll for a bit after your finger leaves the trackpad. If you turn this setting off, the window stops scrolling when you stop touching the trackpad. You'll also see a checkbox for enabling dragging. Check this box and you can choose between two options: with or without Drag Lock. If you enable Drag Lock, you can click something and it will be stuck to your cursor. To drop the item you clicked, simply click again.

If you click the Mouse Options button instead, all you get is a slider for adjusting scrolling speed.

Mouse Keys

Those who have trouble using a mouse or a trackpad can control their cursors with their keyboards instead by heading to this section and turning on Enable Mouse Keys. This is also where you set the length of time you have to hold the directional keys before your cursor starts to move. You can specify the cursor's maximum speed, and the "Ignore built-in trackpad when mouse or wireless trackpad is present" checkbox does just what it says.

Slow Keys

Slow Keys puts a delay between when you press a key and when your Mac acknowledges that you've done so. Turn this feature on and you can adjust that delay period with the Acceptance Delay slider. If your fingers move slowly, this feature can save a lot of unwanted repeated keystrokes. The "Use click key sounds" checkbox tells your Mac to make one sound when you press a key and a different sound when that key press is accepted.

Sticky Keys

For some, pressing the various keystrokes required to operate a Mac can be challenging. Sticky Keys solves this problem. Instead of being forced to hit multiple keys at the same time (such as ⌘ and P to print), Sticky Keys makes your Mac interpret pressing ⌘ and then pressing P the same as if you'd pressed them simultaneously. You'll also find checkboxes that allow you to turn Sticky Keys on or off by tapping the Shift key five times, enable a beep when a modifier key is pressed, and display the pressed keys onscreen as you press them (these last two settings work only if Sticky Keys is enabled).

Speakable Items

This is where you control *speakable items* (short verbal commands you give to your computer like, "What time is it?"). This category has three tabs: Settings, Listening Key, and Commands.

On the Settings tab, the Microphone menu is where you choose which mic to use. You can select one that's plugged into your Mac or go with the built-in mic (assuming your Mac has one). The Calibrate button opens a window where you can practice giving your Mac verbal commands. Use the Upon Recognition settings to make your Mac play a sound to acknowledge that it has received your command (you get to choose the sound).

The Listening Key tab allows you to have the Mac listen either only while you're pressing the Listening Key or after you speak a keyword. (The Change Key button lets you pick which key you press to tell OS X to start listening.) If you decide to go with a keyword, you can choose whether it's optional, and whether it's required before or after the command. The default keyword is "computer," but it's probably wiser to go with a word that you don't say when frustrated (as in "stupid computer!"). "Rosebud" works well; just don't watch *Citizen Kane* while computing.

The Commands tab is where you control exactly what speakables are allowed. In the "Select a command set" list, turn a particular set of commands on or off by checking the box next to it (click the name of a set to see a short explanation of what commands are included in it). For example, you could choose Contacts in the list and then click Configure to see a list of all your contacts. Then you could use speakable commands to tell your Mac to open an email to one of your contacts. Uncheck a particular contact and you won't be able to use speech commands to reach that person. Click the Open Speakable Items Folder button to display, well, the Speakable Items folder. This is where all your speakable actions are stored. You have a bevy of choices built right in, and you can create your own using Automator.

NOTE

If you're going to make your own speakable items, you have to save them in this folder. No big deal, right? In Snow Leopard and earlier versions of OS X, that was true. But in Mountain Lion, the Speakable Items folder is inside your Library folder, which is invisible. So the easiest way to get at this folder to move your own speakables into it is to use the Open Speakable Items Folder button in the Dictation & Speech preference pane.

Startup Disk

The Startup Disk pane lets you specify which currently attached disk you wish to use to start your Mac. You can use any valid startup disk (your choices will show up in the pane), including DVDs and external disks. Clicking Restart reboots your system using the selected disk. (You can also choose a startup disk by pressing and holding the Option key while your Mac is starting).

If your Mac has a FireWire port, you can also choose to start the machine in Target Disk Mode. This turns your high-priced Mac into a glorified hard drive, but it is extremely useful for transferring data and preferences and repairing troublesome hard disks.

Non-Apple Preference Panes

After you install a non-Apple application that has a preference pane of its own, you'll see that pane in a new section of System Preferences labeled Others. These panes work the same as Apple's own—they let you control aspects of the program or feature you added. For example, if you install Perian (*www.perian.org*) so your Mac can display a greater variety of video types, you can adjust Perian via its preference pane.

One of the most common questions about third-party preference panes isn't how to *use* them; it's how to get rid of them. If the third-party application doesn't include an option to uninstall its preference pane, you can manually uninstall the pane by right-clicking or Control-clicking it and then selecting Remove (see Figure 5-8).

Figure 5-8. Removing an unwanted preference pane

NOTE

Removing an application's preference pane removes only the preference pane, not the application itself.

CHAPTER 6

Built-in Applications and Utilities

When you install Mountain Lion, a number of applications and utilities come along for the ride. You get the predictable apps like Safari, and the boring-yet-useful utilities like Activity Monitor, as well as brand-new applications like Reminders. And some of the older applications have been radically upgraded (and, in the case of iChat, renamed; it's now called Messages).

Applications Installed with Mountain Lion

This section gives you a quick rundown of all the applications installed by default with Mountain Lion. Note that the list covers only applications that come with a Mountain Lion install—if you have a brand-new Mac or are upgrading an older Mac, you'll likely have other applications that aren't included in this list (such as iLife).

App Store

The App Store application is Apple's electronic distribution client. If you've used an iOS device or any version of OS X after 10.6.7, you're familiar with the concept. If you haven't used the App Store before, it works like you might expect: When you launch this app, you'll see a store where you can buy a huge variety of apps. The App Store offers recommendations, shows you what's popular, and offers a search function so you can find the perfect app. Once you've made a selection (or several), you type in your iTunes or iCloud password and purchase the chosen app(s).

NOTE

Worried that you could lose the apps you've bought if your computer crashes? Never fear: once you buy an app, you can download it as many times as you like.

Using the Mac App Store differs from the traditional way you're used to managing software. Instead of having to search for updates, you'll find any updates to your purchases prominently indicated in the App Store and in the Notification Center; click Update All to install the latest versions of all your purchases. You can install App Store purchases on any of your authorized Macs (up to five).

NOTE

You can't authorize or deauthorize machines via the Mac App Store. Instead, you have to open iTunes, head up to the Store menu, and then manage your Macs from there using the Authorize/Deauthorize This Computer commands.

Automator

Automator is a workflow tool for automating repetitive tasks: resizing photos, converting files to different types, combining text files, syncing files between folders—that kind of thing. In Mountain Lion, Automator looks and acts much like previous versions, and at first glance you won't notice the difference. But closer inspection reveals new actions that make automating things even easier. So if there was something you couldn't get Automator to do before, now is a great time to revisit this application. Automator supports Auto Save and Versions (see "Auto Save and Versions" on page 92).

Still not finding the script you need? Google has you covered: head to *Google.com* and type "automator actions" into the search box, and you'll find scads of prewritten scripts.

Calculator

When you fire up this application, you get a basic calculator. If you explore the program's menu bar, you'll note that it has scientific and programmer modes (in the View menu), and numerous conversion functions (in the Convert menu). If you want a history of your calculations, you can get a running record by using Paper Tape (⌘-T). Calculator can also speak: the program can announce both button presses and your results; just visit the Speech menu in Calculator's menu bar.

NOTE

Using Calculator for basic math isn't the fastest way to get the answer—Spotlight can do math, too. So if you need a simple expression calculated, type it into Spotlight (see Figure 6-1) and skip Calculator altogether!

Figure 6-1. The same answer as Calculator, but much more convenient

---

Calendar

In earlier versions of OS X your calendaring needs were handled by iCal. You won't find iCal in Mountain Lion because it's been replaced by Calendar. Like iCal, Calendar's interface resembles a desktop calendar, but the program's look is more refined than it was in Lion (see Figure 6-2). Calendar also adds some features not found in the last version of iCal, like a sidebar (click the Calendars button to display it).

Figure 6-2. Rejoice, iCal fans—the sidebar has returned!

Calendar also adds a new method for searching through all your calendar entries: *search tokens*. Search tokens make searching easier. Start typing whatever you're looking for and a list will drop down. When you see what you want, select it from the drop-down menu. The options will be something like the following:

Event contains "scout"
Title
    Scout
Notes
    Scout

Select Scout under Notes and it'll transform into a token. For example, if you search for "Scout" (Figure 6-3) and then select "Scout" under Notes, the calendar is filtered so only entries with "Scout" in their notes show up. You don't have to stop with one token; you can keep adding tokens to find exactly what you want. Search tokens have been around in OS X for some time, but their use is becoming more widespread. For example, you'll now find search tokens in Mail, too.

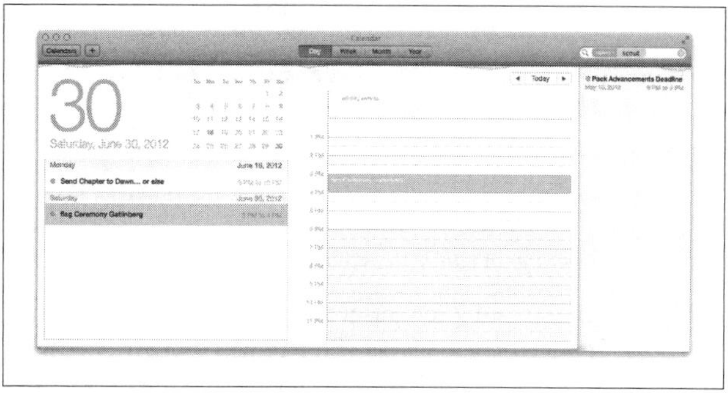

Figure 6-3. Searching Calendar entries

Calendar retains iCal's Quick Event feature—simply click the + button to create an event just by typing the date and time. If your event needs more info than just the day and time, then click the entry and a pop up window will allow you to add alerts, invitees, locations, and so forth (Figure 6-4). If you're subscribed to the invitee's calendar, then clicking Available Meeting Times will reveal any conflicts in your calendar or theirs.

Chess

Mountain Lion features an updated version of Chess. As in earlier versions, you get the standard human-versus-computer chess game, as well as four chess variants, a tweakable board and pieces, and the ability to speak to your Mac to move pieces. (If you don't like the default view, you can change the tilt of the chessboard by clicking and holding the mouse button anywhere on the board's border; arrows will appear that allow you to tilt and rotate the board to your liking.)

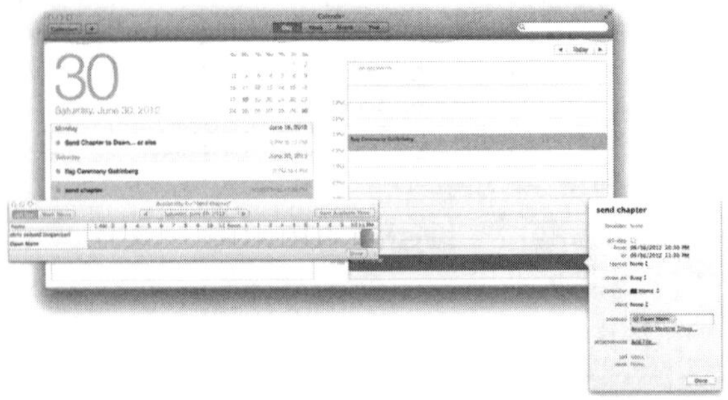

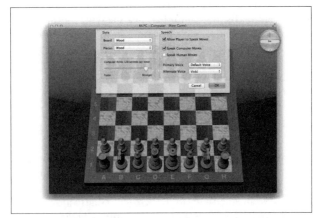

Figure 6-4. Inviting an editor to an event

One difference from previous versions is that the difficulty slider has changed (go to Chess→Preferences to see it). In earlier versions, you just moved the slider to the point where you thought you could beat the computer and then hoped for the best. In this version, the slider is much more informative—it tells you exactly what the computer is doing (Figure 6-5).

Figure 6-5. You're about to get dominated by your Mac

You can also pit the computer against itself or play against another human. Sadly, you can't play chess against someone over a network, so if you want a head-on challenge with a human, they'll have to be at your Mac with you. And if you're suddenly called away from your Mac during a heated game, don't worry —this version of Chess features Auto Save, so you don't have to worry about losing any progress.

The biggest change in Chess? It's included in Game Center (see "Game Center" on page 184), which means your Fisher-esque chess skills will be rewarded with badges!

Contacts

If you look for Address Book in Mountain Lion, you won't find it. The functionality isn't lost, though—the app has been renamed Contacts. But the name isn't the only thing that changed; Contacts includes some upgrades compared with Address Book. For one thing, the three-column layout makes a return after being banished in Lion so you won't have to click that annoying bookmark to flip between individuals and groups of contacts (see Figure 6-6).

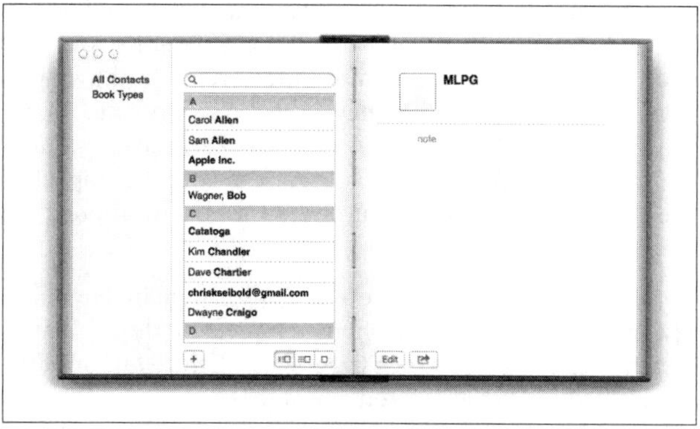

Figure 6-6. The third column for groups is back!

Contacts also features a Share Sheet button so you can easily share a contact via email, Messages, or Air Drop. Like previous versions of Address Book, Contacts stores information in iCloud so if you add or delete a contact on one of your Apple devices, that change shows up on all of them.

NOTE

When you set up your Mac, Contacts automatically adds an entry for you. That might seem crazy—after all, you know how to get in touch with yourself—but there are benefits. For example, you can hit the Share Sheet button in Contacts to easily share your contact info with anyone you wish.

Dashboard

That speedometer-like Dashboard icon that lived in your Dock in Lion is no longer there; it's been replaced by Mission Control. If you were a heavy Dashboard user, don't worry—Dashboard is still on your Mac, you'll just have to hunt it down in the Applications folder. (See "The Dock" on page 73 to learn how to add it to the Dock.)

Dashboard is an environment where mini-applications (called *widgets*) run. When you invoke Dashboard, your Desktop will slide away. And once Dashboard is up and running, the widgets in it will go about doing whatever they're supposed to do (reporting on the weather, displaying a calendar, and so on) until you return to the desktop. To get back to your desktop, click the arrow in the bottom right of the Dashboard or press the Dashboard key again.

Mountain Lion comes with several widgets built in, but only a few will already be in the Dashboard by default: the calculator, weather, calendar, and clock widgets. Click the + button at the Dashboard's lower left to add any of these:

Contacts
Lets you search your Contacts from the Dashboard.

Calculator

This is just a basic calculator; it's much less powerful than the Calculator application built into OS X.

Calendar

Lets you view Calendar events in convenient widget form.

Dictionary

This gives you the same information as the OS X Dictionary application (though without the Wikipedia browsing capabilities). You can use this widget as a dictionary, a thesaurus, or an Apple help interface.

ESPN

Fetches scores and news about your favorite teams.

Flight Tracker

Lets you track flights in real time. If your spouse or roommate is returning from a trip, you can see how long you have left to clean the house.

Movies

Keeps you up to date on the movies playing in your area. Initially, it just cycles through the posters of currently playing movies, but when you click on it, it'll display showtimes and theaters.

Ski Report

Like to ski? This widget keeps you updated on the conditions at your favorite slopes.

Stickies

This is the Dashboard version of Stickies (see "Stickies" on page 205).

Stocks

Got some stocks? Track the roller-coaster ride of investing in the market with this widget.

Tile Game

If you had a pre–OS X Mac, you might remember the game Tile that came as a desk accessory. This is a widgetized version of it. Instead of a picture of the Apple logo, you get to unscramble a picture of a big cat. The tile-scrambling animation is worth watching, even if you never actually play with this widget.

Translation

Translate a word or phrase from one language to another. The shorter the phrase, the more accurate the translation.

Unit Converter

Shouldn't everyone be using SI units by now? Well, probably, but they don't. With this widget, you can discover how many liters there are in an imperial gallon.

Weather

Track the upcoming weather with this widget. You get to choose only one city to track, so if you want to know the weather in more than one place when using Dashboard, you'll need to have multiple Weather widgets running.

Web Clip

Web Clip lets you create your own widgets.

World Clock

If you're using Dashboard all the time and you don't have a watch or you want to know the time in Geneva while you're in San Francisco, this widget has you covered.

Dictionary

This is the dictionary responsible for OS X's system-wide spell-check. When you mistype a word, the suggested spelling appears beneath the word (just like on iOS devices); hit Return to accept the suggestion (don't worry—pressing Return won't add a paragraph break to your document) or just keep typing and OS X will insert the suggestion for you. If you're not happy with OS X's suggestion, then click the tiny × to dismiss it. For spelling that's so bad OS X can't even guess at the word you want, you'll get a dashed red line under the word mocking your ineptitude. Right-click or Control-click words underlined in red to see your Mac's suggestions. If you hate having your words corrected automatically, visit the Language & Text preference pane (see "Language & Text" on page 126) and, on the Text tab, uncheck "Correct spelling automatically."

The Dictionary application is more than just a spellchecker. It also lets you search the *New Oxford American Dictionary*, the *Oxford American Writer's Thesaurus*, Apple's dictionary, and Wikipedia. You can choose which of these four options to use —or search them all at the same time—by clicking the appropriate word near the top of the window (All, Dictionary, and so on). Dictionary is a global application, so you can use it to look up definitions anywhere on your Mac. To do so, select the word in question and then either right-click or Control-click it and choose Look Up "[word]," or use a three-finger double-tap if you have a trackpad capable of understanding that gesture.

DVD Player

DVD Player (surprise!) plays DVDs. If you're upset that Front Row (the program that made video and picture viewing more comfortable in versions of OS X before Lion) isn't included in Mountain Lion, you'll be pleased to learn that DVD Player is a full-screen app, so you can still get that immersive viewing experience when you're watching something intense like *Chairman of the Board*. DVD Player also lets you do things like tweak the video's color or mess with the audio equalizer. And if you've got an Apple remote lying around, you can use it to control DVD Player.

NOTE

By default, DVD Player fires up the movie in Full Screen mode (you can change this behavior by selecting DVD Player→Preferences). Move your mouse to the bottom of the screen to access the playback controls; to the top of the screen to select a chapter; and to the *very* top of the screen to reveal the menu bar, where you can change the size of the playback window.

FaceTime

FaceTime has been fully integrated into Messages and, because it's so convenient, that's likely how you'll access it. But Face-Time is still a stand-alone app, too.

When you first launch FaceTime, you'll be asked to sign in with your Apple ID (or you can create a new account). Once you sign in, you get to decide which email address you want to receive FaceTime calls at. If you have only one address associated with your Apple account, your only option is to click Next; if you have more than one address, click the one you want to use, and then click Next. In the right-hand sidebar, you'll see a scrollable list of your contacts. Click on the person you want to contact and decide if you want to contact her iOS device (iPhone 4 or iPad 2 or newer) or her Mac. For iPads and Macs, you use an email address that the person has set (click it!); for iPhone calls, just click on the number.

Font Book

Font Book gives you control over all the fonts on your Mac. Mountain Lion installs over 100 fonts by default, and other programs may install even more. You can preview, group, install, and deactivate fonts using Font Book, as well as validate fonts to identify any damaged ones that might cause your system to become unstable (go to File→Validate Font). In some cases, duplicate copies of fonts can also cause programs to become unstable. Happily, Font Book lets you deactivate duplicate fonts: go to Edit→Look for Enabled Duplicates. If it finds duplicates, you'll have the choice of resolving them manually or automatically.

Game Center

This is another feature that's been in iOS for some time that is now in OS X. Game Center brings the world of social gaming to your Mac. It lets you compete head to head or cooperatively with your friends (and enemies) in a variety of games. You can also see how your scores stack up, view awards and badges you've earned, and find new games with Game Center.

The Game Center window has four tabs across the top. Here's what they're for:

Me

Clicking this tab tells you all about you. Just log in with your Apple ID, then you can add a picture of yourself from a variety of sources (the stock images that come with Mountain Lion, your albums, or by snapping one with your computer's built-in camera, if it has one) by clicking on the blank Polaroid next to your name. The poker table interface will be littered with icons of your favorite games.

Friends

Here's where you'll find your pals with whom you play games. You'll find a button to Get Friend Recommendations (which are based on people who play the same games as you) and another to Add Friends (either by email address or nickname).

Games

This tab reveals what games Game Center recommends and lists your OS X and iOS games. You'll also find a button labeled Find Game Center Games, which you might imagine brings up a list of Game Center–enabled games in the App Store. It doesn't, it just launches the App Store.

Requests

Here you have a chance to manage (accept or reject) friend requests. You'll also find an Add Friends button that works just like the one on the Friends tab.

Image Capture

Image Capture lets your Mac transfer images from a camera or a scanner. This is useful if you have a bunch of images you need to import from a device to someplace other than iPhoto (which can import images, as well).

iTunes

iTunes started out as a way to manage the music you ripped from your CD library. It does a lot more than that now: it lets you buy music, buy TV shows, rent or buy movies, and, almost incidentally, manage your music, TV shows, podcasts, movies, and iPhone/iPad/iPod Touch App Store purchases. It's also where you control the authorization of your Macs for the Mac App Store (see "App Store" on page 173 for details).

Launchpad

Got an iOS device? If so, Launchpad will seem very familiar; it behaves just like the screen of your iPhone or iPad. For the uninitiated, here's how it works: when you launch Launchpad (by clicking the rocket ship icon in the Dock), your screen fades away and all your applications appear in icon form (Figure 6-7). Launch any one with a single click.

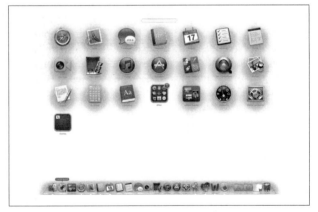

Figure 6-7. It's like you're staring at a giant iPhone

If the only thing you have installed on your Mac is Mountain Lion, all your applications' icons will fit on a single screen. If you've added applications, you'll need more than a single screen to hold them all. Navigating between screens is easy: just two-finger swipe left or right on the trackpad or with a capable mouse to move from page to page.

The application icons are grouped automatically. If you aren't happy with the results, just click an icon, hold your mouse button until all the icons start wiggling, and then drag the icon where you want it to live. (Click any empty spot on the screen to make the icons stop wiggling.) Too many pages of icons? You can create folders. Simply drag one icon on top of another and Launchpad creates a folder containing those applications and gives it a name. If Mountain Lion chooses a poor name for the folder or you just want a snappier one, click the folder to open it and then click its name. Mountain Lion will highlight the name and you'll be able to change it to something else. To delete a folder, open it and then drag the program icons out of it; once there's only a single icon in the folder, the folder disappears.

NOTE

Any folder creation and icon reordering you do in Launchpad is reflected only in Launchpad; the folders and applications remain in the same place when viewed with the Finder.

Surprisingly, you can banish applications from your Mac with Launchpad, though only ones you've purchased from the Mac App Store. To delete applications with Launchpad, press and hold the Option key so all the icons start jiggling. Icons for applications you can delete will have a white × in their top-left corners. Click the × and you'll be warned about deleting the application; confirm your choice and the program is gone. (Deleting an application isn't as permanent as it sounds: since you purchased it from the Mac App Store, you can download it again for free if you ever want it back, though its associated data is gone.)

NOTE

Can't get enough of Launchpad's fade-in animation?
Hold the Shift key when you start Launchpad for a slow-
mo Launchpad experience.

Mail

Mail is the standard email client for OS X. (If you're new to OS
X, skip to the "Adding new accounts" on page 190 to learn
how to get started.) The app, as you can guess, lets you read
and compose emails. But it does a lot more than just that.

One of the new features of Mail is the ability to control what
shows up in Notification Center. By default, any email message
you get shows up in Notification Center. That may seem nifty
at first, but if you get a lot of mail and it's not all high priority,
you likely don't want to be bothered by every single message.
Happily, you can decide exactly which messages show up in
Notification Center. Head to Mail→Preferences and, on the
General tab, you'll discover a drop-down menu labeled "New
message notifications." Clicking this will let you decide which
messages make it through to Notification Center. Your options
are Inbox Only, VIPs, Contacts, All Mailboxes, and any smart
mailboxes you've set up.

Most of those options will be familiar if you've used previous
versions of Mail, but VIPs and Smart Mailboxes are new categories. VIPs are senders you deem important: your spouse, that
cranky uncle who sends you emails with "fwd:fwd:fwd:fwd:"
in the subject line, or your parole officer. To designate someone
a VIP, just open a message from that person and then point
your cursor at her name; you'll see a star magically appear.
Click the star and that person becomes a VIP.

Filtering for VIPs is a nice way to keep Notification Center free
of unwanted notifications, but maybe you want *some*—but not
all—of the mail from certain senders, or want mail about
certain subjects to show up in Notification Center. Smart Mail-

boxes let you do that. To create one, click the tiny + button at the bottom left of the Mail window (if you're using three-column mode) or go Mailbox→New Smart Mailbox A window appears where you can set up all kinds of hoops for a piece of mail to jump through before it makes it to Notification Center (Figure 6-8). Click the + button in this window to add a new criteria.

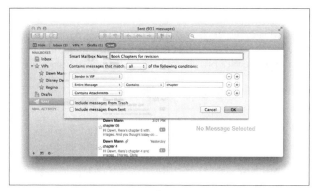

Figure 6-8. Creating a Smart Mailbox that will contain only chapters returned for further editing

You don't have to rely on Smart Mailboxes for your Mail filtering needs, however. Mail still lets you set up rules to handle incoming messages, sending them directly to a destination folder depending on the criteria you select (go to Mail→Preferences→Rules).

For good or ill, you can also create fancy email with Mail by using stationery templates. To access them, click the Stationery button at the top right of any New Message window. Choose one and your mail will be full of color (and probably annoyance) for all the recipients of your missive. If you're looking for an easy way to attach photos to an email (or use them with stationery), Mail includes a browser for all your images stored in iPhoto. In the New Message window, just click the Photo Browser button (it's to the left of the Stationery button) and then choose the picture you want to attach. The following sections contain more info on using Mail.

Adding new accounts

When you first run Mail, it will ask for your name, an existing email address, and the password for that account. (To add another account later, select File→Add Account.) Type in those three bits of information and Mail will try to figure out how to configure your email server. If it can't, it'll ask you to provide detailed settings, such as the incoming server name, account type, and more. You can get that info from your administrator or Internet service provider.

NOTE

If you're just adding an email-only account, Mail is the way to go. But adding accounts with Mail isn't your best option if you're *also* using other services (like chat, calendaring, etc.) offered by your email provider. In that case, head to the Mail, Contacts & Calendars preference pane to take care of everything at once.

Some email services, such as Gmail, allow you to access your mail using either POP (Post Office Protocol) or IMAP (Internet Mail Access Protocol). If you like to access the same email account from multiple devices (such as an iPhone and a computer), IMAP is your best choice, because that way all your mail is stored on the server; when you read a message, it's marked as read across all the devices you access it from. (Some services may *require* you to enable IMAP before you can access them.) To enable IMAP for a service such as Gmail, log into your account using a web browser, and then visit the service's settings page. You may also need to look on the mail service's settings screen or in its help system for instructions on configuring Mail to access it via IMAP.

Add a signature to outgoing mail

You can use a signature to automatically append text or add a picture to the end of your messages. If you end all your emails with the same thing (even if it's only "Thanks, Chris"), a signature can save you some time.

To add a signature, go to Mail→Preferences→Signatures, and then, in the list on the left, choose the account you want to add a signature to (or choose All Signatures to create one for *all* your accounts). Click the + button and then type the signature text into the right-hand box (Mail automatically suggests your name and email address, but you can just type over that). If you want to use an image (such as a picture of your *actual* signature), scan it in, whittle it down to a small size (you can use Preview to do that), save the image as a file, then drag the image file into the right-hand box. If you add more than one signature, you can click the Choose Signature drop-down menu in this window and then specify a signature or tell Mail to rotate through your signatures sequentially or randomly.

Enable junk mail filtering

Head to Mail→Preferences→Junk Mail, and then make sure the box next to "Enable junk mail filtering" is checked. You can have Mail leave the suspected junk in your inbox or move it to the Junk mailbox. Note that every time you mark a message as junk, Mail learns from your action and improves its junk filtering. But Mail's junk filter isn't 100 percent accurate, so if all your email providers offer their own junk filtering, you might not want to bother with Mountain Lion's junk filtering, too.

Add a mailbox

To add a new, standard mailbox, go to Mailbox→New Mailbox. To add a Smart Mailbox—which lets you set criteria for messages that should go straight into it (without you having to lift a finger)—choose New Smart Mailbox instead, and you'll be presented with a window where you can set your criteria.

Quickly delete junk mail

If you've become confident in Mail's ability to figure out which mail is junk, you can get rid of those messages by pressing Option-⌘-J or going to Mailbox→Erase Junk Mail.

Search your mail

You can use Spotlight to search for that elusive memo you want to reread, but if you use the search box in Mail's menu bar, you won't have to wade through search results from other sources. You'll get the same lightning-fast results, but you'll see only matches from your email, notes, and to-dos.

Messages

You won't find iChat anywhere in Mountain Lion because it's been replaced by the more ambitious Messages, which retains all the functionality of iChat and adds more options for communicating with others.

After you launch Messages, you can set up an account using any of the standard chat protocols found on the Mac by clicking the + button in the lower-left side of the window; your options are AIM, Jabber, Google Talk, and Yahoo. (If you use iCloud, this info is already available once you sign into your account, so you won't see this button.) Once you set up your accounts, you can use Messages just as you used iChat.

As you'd expect, you can do more with Messages than just instant-message people. You can send a text to a buddy, start a video chat with FaceTime, or have a three-way meeting. Messages rolls all your communication into one simple-to-use app.

Mission Control

In a nutshell, Mission Control is a window-management application that was introduced in Lion. But that description, while accurate, is far too terse. Mission Control is composed

---

of Spaces (virtual desktops for your different workflow needs; "Spaces" has details), Dashboard for the information that you want quick access to (see "Dashboard"), full-screen applications, and the regular windowed applications you know and love. That's four distinctly different ways of interacting with your Mac.

Switching between a full-screen application and the desktop used to be cumbersome, but Mission Control fixes that. Instead of forcing you to click and hunt for minimized windows, Mission Control puts everything that's running on your Mac into one easy-to-navigate window. For example, if you happen to be writing a book, launching Mission Control might reveal a monitor that looks like Figure 6-9.

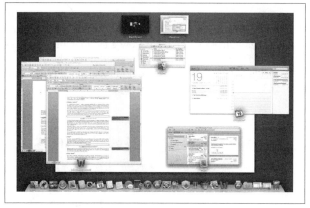

Figure 6-9. It's all right in front of you!

You launch Mission Control by either pressing F3 (on most keyboards) or swiping up with three fingers on your trackpad (you can adjust this in the Mission Control preference pane; see "Mission Control" on page 126). When you invoke Mission Control, you see Dashboard, your desktop, Spaces, and any open full-screen apps across the top. Normal application windows appear in the center of the screen (grouped by application), and the Dock is where it normally is.

Once Mission Control is active, you can add desktop spaces by dragging a window from the center of your screen to the upper-right corner of the screen (a + sign will appear). To add an empty desktop space, move your cursor to that same corner and click the +. To delete a space, put your cursor over it and click the × that appears.

Once you decide where you want to go (that pesky game of Angry Birds or the book you're writing, say), just click the window you want to jump to. Swipes also work if you're using a trackpad: a quick swipe to the left or right will switch between applications.

Notes

In previous versions of OS X, notes you created on your iOS device showed up in Mail, which was clunky and a bit confusing. In Mountain Lion, Notes is now a standalone app (Figure 6-10). Type up a note on your iPhone and it shows up on your Mac in a minute or two. You don't have to stick to plain ol' text, either: Notes can handle video, rich text, and audio as well.

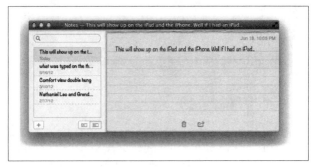

Figure 6-10. Making one note that will show up everywhere

Notes is simple to use. The controls live at the bottom of the window. The + button creates a new note, and the two window buttons toggle between a three- and two-column view. To delete a note, click the trash can icon, and to share a note click the Share Sheet button.

Photo Booth

Photo Booth is likely the silliest and most fun application included with Mountain Lion. It lets you do things as simple as snapping a picture with your Mac's built-in iSight camera and as complicated as filming a short movie with a fake background. PhotoBooth even allows you to trim clips by picking the starting and ending frames. And Mountain Lion makes it easier than ever to share your creations.

Photo Booth is now full screen by default, but you aren't stuck in full-screen mode. Move your cursor to the top of the window and click on the arrows in the blue rectangle that appear in the upper-right corner or hit Esc to use Photo Booth on the desktop. No matter which view you choose, the area below the photo is where your options for creating something great live.

On the far left, you'll find three buttons. From left to right, they allow you to take four quick shots, take a single snap, and make a movie, respectively. In the center of the strip, you'll see a big red button with an icon on it of either a camera (for snaps) or a video camera (for movies). Clicking this, as you'd expect, takes the photo or starts recording the movie. And on the far left side you'll find the Effects button.

The Effects button is the most interesting (and fun) thing to play with. Clicking it lets you choose from 36 preset effects and create eight custom backdrops (to create a custom backdrop, drag a picture or a movie onto one of the User Backdrop X squares). The effects range from weird distortions (Alien), to comical (Dizzy), to built-in green-screening. The green-screening options are on the fourth page of effects; if you select one of those (or one of the custom backdrops you created), your Mac will ask you to step out of the frame and, when you re-enter the frame, it will look like you're in front of one of the stock backdrops or one you created.

NOTE

If you want to use backdrops for your Photo Booth creations, make sure that there's a lot of contrast between you and what's behind you. Otherwise, Photo Booth probably won't do a great job of replacing your real-life backdrop with the one you chose.

After you take a picture or make a video, you'll find your creation in the bottom of the Photo Booth window. Click the image you're interested in and you'll discover yet another Share Sheet button (another Mountain Lion improvement). You can share your pic in a variety of ways, from email to Twitter. Or, to delete a pic or video, click the × in its upper right.

Preview

Preview is the default image viewer for Macs; any image you download in a common format such as *.jpg*, *.png*, or *.pdf* will open in it. Preview lets you resize, crop, and annotate images and adjust their colors. You can also use it to snap screenshots, create icons, and more.

The most exciting thing about Preview? It's now in the cloud (Figure 6-11). That's right: when you open Preview, you'll get a chance to decide where you want your creations to live. Anything you put on iCloud you'll be able to access anywhere at any time.

The version of Preview that ships with Mountain Lion doesn't offer a lot of new tools, but it does change where you find its tools. Instead of having, say, the thought-bubble tool as part of a drop-down menu, you'll now find it in the toolbar at the top of the image. To display this toolbar, click the Show Edit Toolbar button, which looks like a pencil top and a piece of paper.

Figure 6-11. Preview is in the cloud

QuickTime Player

QuickTime is the technology behind much of OS X's media savvy: DVD Player, iTunes, and other applications rely heavily on it. You can use QuickTime Player to watch movies and listen to music, and it's also useful for generating quick audio or visual content. You can record directly into QuickTime via your iSight camera, attached webcam, or microphone, and then use the program to perform simple trimming. Once you've created something you want to share with the world, you can post it directly from QuickTime to a variety of destinations via the Share menu.

There's one other killer feature in QuickTime: the ability to record your screen. Choose File→New Screen Recording, click the red circle in the middle of the window that appears, and you'll be off to the wonderful world of screencasting.

Reminders

Reminders isn't brand new—you've seen it in iOS—but it *is* new to OS X. And it's a very welcome addition. Reminders is a simple but extremely useful app. To create a task (like "Write book"), click the + button in the program's upper-right corner, and Reminders will add an entry for that task. Put your cursor over the entry and you'll see an "i"; click it and you'll be able assign a date and/or location when you want to be reminded of that task, control whether the task repeats, set its priority level, and add a note to it.

That explains how to set up something in Reminders but leaves you wondering what will happen when it's time for you to be reminded. Exactly how you are reminded depends on what device you're using. Imagine your child's birthday is coming up. You walk by a toy store on your way to work every day, so you set up a reminder on your Mac to let you know when you're at the toy store (Figure 6-12). When you approach the toy store, you'll be reminded via the Notification Center on your Mac, iPad, or iPhone (or all three if you roll that way) depending on how you've set up the notifications on your Mac/iPhone/iPad. You can adjust these settings in the Notifications preference pane (see "Notifications" on page 134). (Note that, while your device is happy to remind you to make a purchase at the toy store, it won't really help you if you secretly bought that Lego set for yourself.)

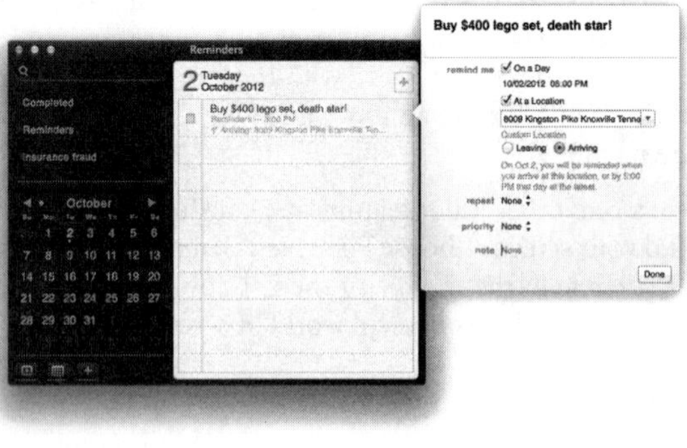

Figure 6-12. Reminders to the location-specific rescue!

You aren't stuck with just one list—you can create separate lists so related tasks are grouped together. To make a new list, click the + button in the lower-left corner of the window and Notes adds a list named New List; simply start typing to re-name it.

Once you've completed a task, click the box next to it in the list and that task will get moved to the Completed list.

Safari

Safari is the slick web browser that comes with OS X. Safari has undergone some big changes in Mountain Lion, but if you've used previous versions of the program, you'll be able to use this version without much effort.

The biggest change is the lack of a search field. Does this mean you have to go to Google every time you want to search for something? Of course not. The search field and the URL field have been united: Just start typing in that field—which says "Search Google or enter an address"—and you'll see a drop-down list appear (Figure 6-13). You can select any of the list's options, which include Google search results that match what you've typed, items from your browsing history, and the option to just go to the URL you've typed. If it seems tedious to select from all those options, you'll be happy to know that you don't have to; just type in what you're looking for and then hit Re-turn; Safari selects the highlighted option (and it's pretty good at guessing what you want).

NOTE

If you want Safari to give you search results from Yahoo or Bing instead of Google, go to Safari→Preferences and, on the General tab, choose a different option from the "Default search engine" menu.

Another change for Safari is that your tabs are now stored in iCloud. That means you can click the Cloud button next to the Forward and Back arrow buttons and Safari will show you all

---

Figure 6-13. Using Safari's unified search and URL bar

the tabs open on all your other devices when iOS 6 is released. This can be super handy when you've found a great website on your laptop at home and then want to view it on your iMac at work—no more emailing URLs to yourself!

Next to the Cloud button is a Share Sheet button. Click this and you'll be able to quickly add the current page to your reading list, create a bookmark for it, or share it in a variety of ways.

NOTE

It's worth taking a moment to familiarize yourself with the most common uses of "read" when it comes to Safari. The most obvious is Safari Reader. You'll see a Reader button on the right side of the address/search field; clicking it leaves you with just a black-and-white text version of the website you're viewing, with no animations or ads (this feature is available only on text-based sites). And when you click the Share Sheet button, one of your options is "Add to Reading List." Safari's Reading List is for marking pages that you want to read later, it's like a bookmark but without the heavy commitment. To see the items in your Reading List, click the eyeglasses icon.

There are a few other, smaller changes. Apple removed Safari's RSS reader function, so if you enjoy RSS, you'll need to find a third-party option like NetNewsWire (it's available from the App Store). And tabs don't have a maximum size anymore—they stretch to fill the width of your Safari window.

There's one more change to Safari that you'll love: the new Cover Flow method for flipping through your open tabs. Just click the rightmost tab and you'll be scrolling through your open tabs in Cover Flow fashion! (See "Finder views" on page 64 for more on Cover Flow View.)

Even with these changes, Safari is still the browser you're used to. It's built on the open source WebKit browser platform (*www.webkit.org*), and is both full-featured and web standards–compliant. There's a lot to Safari: it does everything you expect from a web browser and a little more, so getting it set up the way you want it is worth the effort. The following sections explain some of your options.

Change the home page

When you get a new Mac, the default home page is *www.apple.com*. This is great if you love to keep up with Apple, but probably a bit boring for everyday use. To set a new home page, go to Safari→Preferences→General, and then type the URL of the page you want in the Homepage text box or, if you've already loaded the page you want, click "Set to Current Page."

Change the default browser

If you'd like to use a browser other than Safari (such as Firefox) by default, head to Safari→Preferences→General, and then choose the browser you want from the "Default web browser" pop-up menu.

Control which pages are shown in Top Sites

Safari 5 features a slick splash page, Top Sites, that includes snapshots of your most commonly visited sites. (To see it, either press Shift-⌘-1 or click the icon below the left side of the address bar that looks like a bunch of tiny squares.) It's useful and visually appealing, but Safari might include some pages there that you don't want to see. You can edit which pages are shown by clicking the Edit button in the lower-left corner of the Top Sites screen. Lock down pages you want to keep by clicking their pushpin icons, and banish pages you don't want shown by clicking their ×'s. (A blue star in the corner of a web page means the page has been updated since your last visit.)

You can add a page directly to Top Sites by choosing Bookmarks→Add Bookmark and then choosing Top Sites from the menu that appears. (Note that Top Sites bookmarks aren't synced to iCloud, so you should save the URL somewhere in your Bookmarks bar or Bookmarks menu, as well.)

Find a page you didn't bookmark

It happens to everyone: you see an interesting site but don't bother to bookmark it, and then three days later you want to go back to that site but don't remember what it's called or how you ended up on it. Safari's browsing history to the rescue! To bring up your history, select History→Show All History or click Top Sites and then click the History button near the top of the screen). Then type whatever snippet you remember about the mystery site in the search box. Safari returns all the web pages that you've been to that contain what you searched for.

Block pop-up ads

This feature is enabled by default, but after some annoying site asks you to turn it off, you can re-enable pop-up blocking by going to Safari→Block Pop-Up Windows (Shift-⌘-K). A check-mark next to that menu item indicates that the pop-up blocker is active.

Change where downloaded items are saved

By default, Safari saves downloaded items in the Downloads folder in your Home directory, but you can have Safari download to any spot you like. Go to Safari→Preferences→General and then, in the "Save downloaded files to" pop-up menu, click Other and choose a new location.

Control cookies

Most websites send cookies (small bundles of data that are stored between sessions and visits to a website) to your browser. If you're concerned about how cookies are used, you can customize the way Safari handles them. Click Safari→Preferences→Privacy, and then choose the setting you want in the "Block cookies" section. You can also examine all the cookies that Safari has by clicking Details. From there, you can search, view, and remove cookies. To remove all cookies in one fell swoop, click Remove All Website Data.

Get rid of Safari's history

You might find yourself on sites that you don't really want to be on, but Safari isn't picky and saves *all* the sites you visit in its history. Although there are some things that, once seen, cannot be unseen, you may still like to pretend that you never visited a particular site. If so, you can either delete Safari's entire history (go to History→Clear History) or delete offending entries by hand (go to History→Show All History, select the site[s] you want to get rid of, and then hit the Delete key).

If you do nothing, Safari will automatically delete your browsing history after one year. If this interval is too long or too short for your taste, you can change its duration by adjusting Safari's preferences. Take a trip to Safari→Preferences→General and change the "Remove history items" setting. You can choose preset intervals between one day and one year or take control of the situation and select Manually.

Add a URL to the desktop

If you like to have sites you frequently visit accessible directly from your desktop, highlight the URL of the site you want in Safari's address bar and then drag the URL directly onto the desktop. Alternatively, you can drag a site's favicon (the icon to the left of the page's address) instead. Either way, a file icon appears on your desktop with the URL or page's title as its name. Now you can double-click this icon to load that page in your default browser. To change the name of the icon, click its name and then type something more meaningful, just as you would with any other file.

Browse privately

There are times when you don't want Safari keeping track of your history; Private Browsing is the answer. To turn it on, click Safari→Private Browsing. The dialog box that appears details what Private Browsing does. Click OK to browse without having your searches remembered, sites you visit added to Safari's history, or cookies stored permanently.

NOTE

Private Browsing isn't a "set it and forget it" option; it applies only to your current session. So if you quit Safari, the next time you open it, Private Browsing will be inactive and Safari will diligently record all your online comings and goings.

Turn off Autofill

Autofill is a great timesaver, although it's a bit of a security risk if you leave your Mac unattended while you're logged in (for a tip on making that a little safer, see "Password Management" on page 218). To get Safari to *not* automatically enter your login information for websites, go to Safari→Preferences→AutoFill, and uncheck the box next to "User names and passwords."

Customize Safari's toolbar

Safari's default toolbar is missing some buttons you might want, such as a Home button to take you to your home page. You can add buttons to Safari's toolbar by going to View→Customize Toolbar and then dragging the buttons you want right onto the toolbar. While the Customize Toolbar pane is open, you can also get rid of the things you don't want on Safari's toolbar by dragging them off of it, and rearrange toolbar items by dragging them around.

Stickies

Stickies are virtual Post-it notes. Fire up this application and you can leave notes all over your desktop. Select File→New or press ⌘-N to create a blank note you can type in, add images to, and use for reminders. When the list on a sticky becomes something you need to share, you can export it as rich text by choosing File→Export Text.

System Preferences

This is the place to tweak OS X. System Preferences are covered in Chapter 5.

TextEdit

TextEdit is a not-too-shabby word processor that you can use to write the great American novel or a grocery list. Although earlier versions of TextEdit were limited, it keeps gaining features in every new version of OS X. For example, TextEdit now takes advantage of iCloud. That's right: you can store your TextEdit documents in the cloud and work on them from any of your devices!

Mountain Lion's system-wide spellchecker is available in the program, and you can also add a grammar check (select TextEdit→Preferences and turn on "Check grammar with spelling"). TextEdit's default format for saving files is *.rtf* (Rich Text Format), but you can also save (and open) HTML; OpenOffice.org (*.odt*); and Microsoft Word 97, 2003, and 2007 documents. TextEdit can also open and save *.docx* (Word 2011) files, but you might lose some formatting or comments when you open one; saving as a *.docx* file preserves the formatting from TextEdit.

NOTE

You can even add text styles in TextEdit: select some text and then use the Format menu to make it look the way you want. Then click the Styles button at the top left of the editing window (the button has a ¶ symbol on it), choose Show Styles, and then click "Add to Favorites" (Figure 6-14). You'll then be able to give the file a name for future use.

Time Machine

Time Machine automates the backing-up process and puts a beautiful graphical interface on flipping back time. To use Time Machine, all you really need is an attached drive with sufficient space, another Mac, or Time Capsule (Apple's all-in-one backup device and WiFi router).

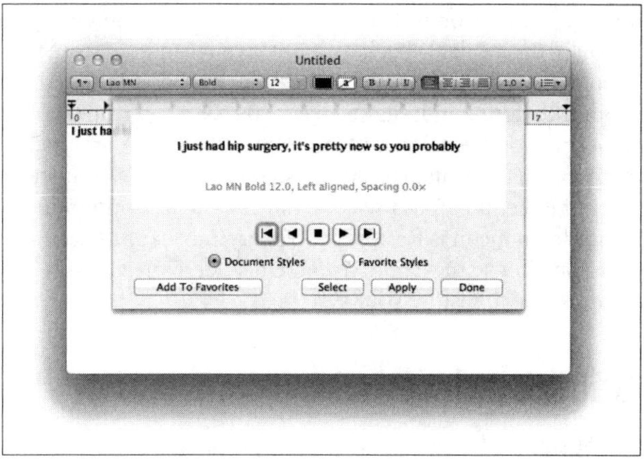

Figure 6-14. TextEdit styles in action

NOTE

Alas, you can't plug a hard drive into an AirPort base station and use Time Machine on that disk. Your choices are limited to another Mac, Time Capsule, or an attached drive.

Time Machine operates seamlessly once it's set up and turned on. To set it up, connect a suitable drive, and then launch Time Machine (Applications→Time Machine), click Set Up Time Machine, and then choose which disk (or Time Capsule) you want to use as a Time Machine disk. After Time Machine is up and running, you can make a few adjustments. When you launch Time Machine, you'll see a big On/Off button, a button to bring up the Select Disk dialog box, and an Options button. Clicking the Options button lets you specify which folders and drives you *don't* want backed up; just click the + button in the dialog box that appears and then select the items you want to exclude.

Using Time Machine is intuitive when you're looking for a file you accidentally deleted (click the Time Machine menu extra or application icon to launch the program, and then navigate through the available backups). But if you want to restore your system from a Time Machine backup, you'll first need to boot from the Mountain Lion Recovery 10.8 (see "Startup trouble-shooting" on page 114). Once you've booted up and picked your installation language, don't start installing OS X. Instead, click the menu bar and select Utilities. The last option in the drop-down menu is Restore System From Backup; selecting it lets you choose the Time Machine disk or Time Capsule you want to use to restore your system.

Utilities Included with Mountain Lion

What's the difference between an application and a utility? It's largely semantic. Utilities are a *type* of application, but in general the ones called "applications" allow you to create and modify data, while the ones called "utilities" allow you to monitor and manage your Mac. There's a reason Utilities is a subfolder of Applications and not the other way around: utilities usually aren't as exciting as the applications you find in the rest of the Applications folder.

But that doesn't mean the Utilities folder is full of arcane, boring stuff. There are plenty of useful applications inside. You'll imagine great uses for a lot of them once you get a quick peek at what they do.

Activity Monitor

The main window of Activity Monitor includes a list of all the processes running on your Mac (click a column heading to change how the list is sorted). You can view stats about CPU load, system memory, disk activity, disk usage, or your network by clicking the various buttons near the bottom of the window. Click a process in the list and then click the Inspect icon to get a closer look at that process. You can also use Activity Monitor to quit any process by selecting the process and then clicking the Quit Process icon (very useful when a program is needlessly hogging the processor or is unresponsive).

NOTE

If Activity Monitor is running, it can display a constantly running graph of system usage in the Dock. You can control what data is being displayed by right-clicking on the Dock icon and choosing the data you want Disk Utility to display in the Dock.

AirPort Utility

If you own a Time Capsule, an AirPort base station, or an AirPort Express, you can use this utility to manage those devices.

AppleScript Editor

AppleScript is a programming language that's designed to be easy to use. It can control scriptable applications on your Mac (that includes most, but not all, applications), allowing you to generate scripts that can, for example, resize photos automatically. Using the AppleScript Editor lets you write, edit, test, run, and compile AppleScripts. For more information, see *http://developer.apple.com/applescript*.

Audio MIDI Setup

MIDI is an acronym for Musical Instrument Digital Interface. This utility lets you hook musical instruments up to your computer, which is useful for fans of GarageBand and other audio programs.

Bluetooth File Exchange

Use this utility to send files to supported Bluetooth devices, such as phones, PDAs, or other computers. (Bluetooth is slower than WiFi but requires less setup to transfer files.) After you launch this utility, you can either drag the file you want to transfer onto the Bluetooth Dock icon and wait for a list of recipients to appear, or select a file in the Bluetooth File Exchange window and then click the Send button (and wait for the list of possible recipients to appear).

Boot Camp Assistant

Boot Camp Assistant lets you install Windows (XP, Vista, or 7) on any Mac running Mountain Lion. This utility will partition your hard drive and install the necessary drivers. (Obviously, you'll need a Windows installation disk.) Once Boot Camp Assistant works its magic, you'll have a dual-boot Mac capable of running Mountain Lion or Windows. You choose which operating system to boot into using the Startup Disk preference pane—see "Startup Disk" on page 169.

NOTE

Boot Camp isn't the only way to get Windows onto your Mac. There are several third-party programs that let you run Windows and Mountain Lion at the same time (as opposed to Boot Camp, which requires you to reboot when you want to switch operating systems). Two popular ones are Parallels Desktop and VMware Fusion.

ColorSync Utility

Because everyone sees colors a little differently and devices often interpret colors in different ways, ColorSync helps you manage colors. It lets you repair ICC (International Color Consortium) profiles on your Mac (click the Profile First Aid icon to do so). Click the Profiles icon to inspect the profiles used by your Mac; ColorSync displays a groovy 3-D plot of the profile you select (when applicable). The Devices icon lets you manage the profiles of attached devices. ColorSync Utility also allows you to apply filters to, for example, a PDF document with the Filters icon. Finally, the Calculator icon lets you sample any pixel displayed on your computer and find its values (click the magnifying glass icon and then click the color you're interested in).

Console

Unlike your car keys, your Mac keeps track of itself. Every time something unexpected (or even routine) happens, the system notes it in a log, but these logs are a bit difficult to find. That's where Console comes in: it lets you review the errors logged on your Mac much more conveniently than if you had to dig through the Library folder. Clicking on the Show/Hide Log List icon toggles a sidebar showing the logs available on your computer. The logs contain information critical for diagnosing bugs you send to Apple and can be useful in tracking a problematic application.

NOTE

If you open Console, don't be alarmed by the number of messages you see; OS X just logs a lot of information. You can use the search box to find what you're looking for, or click a specific item in the Log List sidebar to filter out the unwanted information.

DigitalColor Meter

With this utility, you can inspect the color values of anything displayed onscreen. You can set the size of the aperture (all the way down to a single pixel) and choose from five different ways the results can be calculated.

Disk Utility

Disk Utility is a toolbox for all your disks. You can use it to erase disks (including CD-RWs and DVD-RWs), format disks, mount and unmount disks (if you've ejected an attached disk, you can remount it without unplugging/replugging it by clicking Disk Utility's Mount icon), securely delete data, create compressed or uncompressed disk images, repair permissions, partition disks, and more. To learn how to use Disk Utility to check your drive's health, see the section "Startup Problems" on page 111.

NOTE

Most disks come formatted for Windows computers. While these disks will work with your Mac, it's a good idea to use Disk Utility to change the disk's format to OS X's native Mac OS Extended (Journaled) filesystem, because some features, like Time Machine, won't work with a Windows-formatted disk.

Grab

Grab is OS X's screen-capture utility. It lets you capture a section of the screen, a complete window (sans drop shadow), or the entire screen. It even has a timed option that gives you 10 seconds to get whatever process you're trying to capture running. All the images are saved in *.tiff* format.

Grapher

Grapher displays graphs of equations that are built into the program, as well as equations you enter. This utility can handle a wide range of coordinate choices (polar, cylindrical, Cartesian, and spherical), and can even generate 3-D graphs. This is a useful tool if you're studying calculus.

Java Preferences

This utility is where you tell your Mac what you want the Java programming language to do for you and how. It lets you select your preferred version of Java, manage security, and configure debugging.

Keychain Access

Keychain Access stores your passwords for the moments when you inevitably forget them. As long as you remember your system password, you can recover any password stored in the Keychain. (Many third-party programs, like Firefox, don't use Keychain.) You can also create secure notes readable only in Keychain that are locked with your password. For more on Keychain Access, see Chapter 7.

Migration Assistant

When you first set up your Mac, you had the option of transferring your data from another computer. You were also assured that if you didn't want to transfer your data right then, you could do it later. For more info on all the ways you can transfer data using Migration Assistant, see "Moving Data and Applications" on page 23.

Network Utility

Network Utility lets you perform common networking tasks. Most users will find the Info tab the most useful. For those familiar with Unix network diagnostics, there are also tabs for Netstat, Ping, Lookup, Traceroute, Whois, Finger, and Port Scan.

RAID Utility

Got a RAID (redundant array of inexpensive disks) card installed in your Mac? No? Then you can ignore this utility. If you *do* have a RAID card, this utility lets you configure a RAID on your system.

System Information

This utility can tell you just about everything you might want to know about your Mac. Hardware, networks, and software

are all covered in great detail. If you're wondering about any particular aspect of your Mac, then System Information is the place to look.

Terminal

OS X is built on Unix, and the Terminal utility is your window into that world. Unix is incredibly powerful and Terminal lets you run Unix commands. Clicking Help→Terminal Help will get you started if you aren't familiar with Unix. The most important Terminal tip? When you're confused, typing `man com mand-name` brings up a manual page where you can learn about a particular Unix command (try `man man` for starters). If you like, you can make Terminal full screen by clicking the arrows in the upper right.

Most Mac owners avoid Terminal because the idea of typing commands seems archaic. Surprisingly, there's plenty of fun to be had in Terminal. Try opening Terminal and typing this:

```
telnet towel.blinkenlights.nl
```

VoiceOver Utility

VoiceOver is OS X's screen-reading program that describes what's happening on your screen using one of the voices installed with OS X. This utility allows you to customize VoiceOver's settings: you can control which voice it uses, how your computer is navigated when using VoiceOver, how VoiceOver handles web pages, and how the keys on the keyboard control your Mac. You can even set up a Braille monitor. For additional information, see "VoiceOver" on page 165.

X11

This looks like a utility, but it isn't. Instead, double-clicking this will open up a window asking you if you want to be taken to a site to get X11 software. If you click Continue, you'll be taken to the home of XQuartz software, which offers software

---

you'll want to install if you want to use a program that doesn't support standard OS X windowing. One example of this is the open-source image editor called GIMP. While your Mac can run the program's code, GIMP doesn't use the same windowing system used by OS X, so if you want to run it, you'll need a version of X11.

CHAPTER 7

Managing Passwords in Mountain Lion

When you first boot a new Mac and set up a user, the system is configured to automatically log in that user. That's probably fine if you're the only person who uses that computer, but not so great if your Mac is sitting out where a lot of people have access to it. You'll want to customize your security settings to fit the environment where you'll be using your Mac. If it's a desktop machine and you'll be using it only at home, for example, you probably don't have much to worry about. But if it's a MacBook that you plan on hauling everywhere you go, you'll want a little more security.

NOTE

See "Logging In" on page 42 to find out how to disable automatic login, and see "Logging Out, Sleeping, and Shutting Down" on page 43 to customize your logout options.

Security in OS X usually comes down to passwords: passwords for services, accounts, websites, and email. Once you've created all those pesky but necessary passwords, you'll want to turn your attention to managing them.

Password Management

To manage all your passwords, Mountain Lion uses keychains; they're where it stores your passwords and certificates to keep them safe from prying eyes. These keychains save you a lot of time, because your Mac can use the stored passwords to do a variety of useful things, like joining your wireless network without any help from you.

The more you do online, the more passwords you need. Ideally, you want different passwords for everything; using the same password for your bank's website and for posting to a third-rate message board isn't the best idea. However, with so many passwords running around, it is easy to forget them. We've all been faced with the situation where we were *sure* we typed in the right password, only to be repeatedly denied access. Fortunately, OS X can help.

Recovering a Forgotten Password

So you've forgotten the password to some rarely visited yet essential server or some network you join only every six months. Turns out Mountain Lion probably remembered the password *for* you because chances are good that when you first entered the password, Mountain Lion asked if you wanted it to save the password, you chose Yes. (The three options are Yes, Never, and Not Now; since Yes is the default, that's the option most people choose.) To recover the password, open Keychain Access (Applications→Utilities→Keychain Access) and then type the name of the site or application, or something else relevant into the program's search box. Keychain Access will find entries that match your search criteria and present you with a list like the one in Figure 7-1.

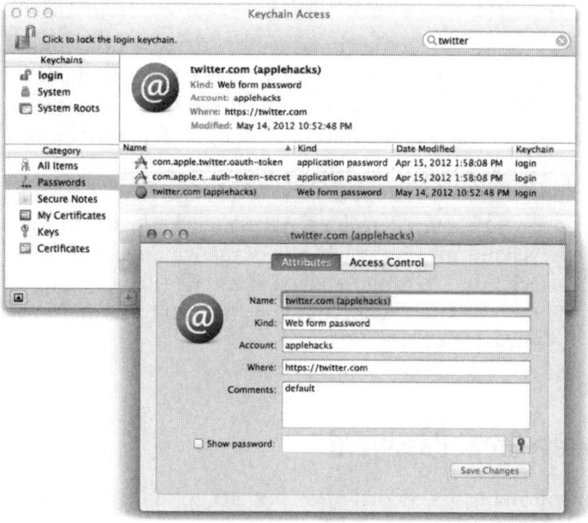

Figure 7-1. Recovering a Twitter password

When whatever you're looking for appears in the list in the middle of the Keychain Access window, double-click that item and a window will pop up that includes a "Show password" checkbox. Check the box, enter your keychain password (usually, but not necessarily, the same as your OS X password), and you'll see the password.

For an added level of security, you can configure OS X to lock your keychain after a period of inactivity. Open Keychain Access, click "login" in the Keychains list on the left side of the window, and then select Edit→"Change Settings for Keychain 'login.'" You'll then be able to lock the keychain after a period of inactivity or when the computer sleeps. Once a keychain is locked, Mountain Lion won't let your Mac give out passwords until you unlock the keychain by typing in your password.

NOTE

If you work on a Mac managed by someone other than
yourself, you probably don't want your keychain password to be the same as your OS X password. Why? Because, if the administrator set your OS X password for
you, that person will also be able to access the information that's on your keychain. To change your keychain
password, open Keychain Access, click "login" in the
Keychains list on the left side of the window, and then
select Edit→"Change Password for Keychain 'login.'"
Enter a new password and your data will be safe from
everyone but you.

Make a Great Password

The following passwords are not acceptable: *letmein*, *password*, *123*, and *qwerty*. Using one of those for anything you
care about is like leaving the door to your house wide open—
but removing the welcome mat. Sure, a miscreant *might* pause
momentarily when he notices the mat is missing, but that won't
stop him from coming into your house. You need a better
password.

Mountain Lion can help you in your quest. You can find out
whether your chosen password is strong with Password Assistant, which tests password strength. For whatever reason, you
can't access Password Assistant directly—you have to use Keychain Access to get to it. (Actually, any prompt that displays
the little key icon will give you access to Password Assistant,
but Keychain Access is one of the easiest ways to get there.)
Open Keychain Access (Applications→Utilities→Keychain Access), and then select Edit→"Change Password for Keychain
'[keychain name].'"

In the dialog box that pops up, type a prospective password in
the New Password field. As you type, you'll see a colored bar
appear that indicates how good your password is (red for weak,
yellow for fair, and green for good or excellent). Under that is

a Password Strength rating (Weak, Fair, Good, or Excellent). When you're done typing, click the key icon and the Password Assistant window appears (Figure 7-2).

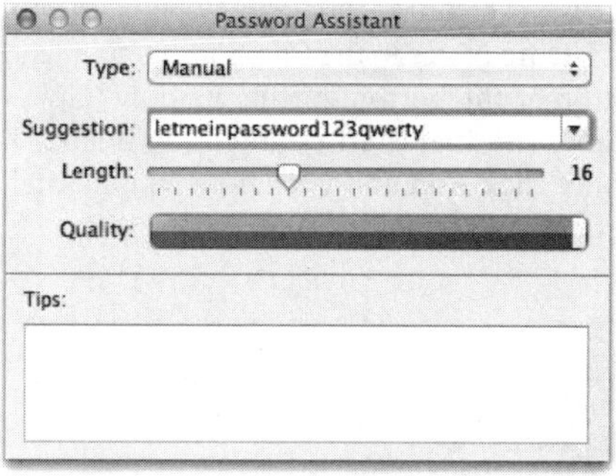

Figure 7-2. Know your password's strength

If your password isn't the digital equivalent of Fort Knox, try out some new passwords in the Password Assistant window to see how they rate. If you can't come up with a good one on your own, Mountain Lion is happy to pitch in and help. The Password Assistant window's Tips field gives you pointers on how to build a better password, and the Type drop-down menu lets you choose the kinds of passwords Mountain Lion suggests: "memorable" ones, ones with letters and numbers, purely numeric ones, random ones, or FIPS 181–compliant ones (the kind used by government agencies).

Once you've found a good, strong password, close the Password Assistant window and then click Cancel in the "Enter a new password for..." window (unless you actually want to change the password for that keychain). Now you can type that password into whatever program or website needs it and know that your info should be pretty secure.

Storing Secure Notes

Keychain is great at storing passwords, but you can also use it to store notes. To write a note that no one else can see (well, except for people who know your OS X username and password), open Keychain Access, click "login" in the Keychains list, select Secure Notes in the Category section, and then click the + button at the bottom of the window. Give your secret note a name, and then start typing away (Figure 7-3). When you're done, click Add and your note will be safely stored in that Keychain.

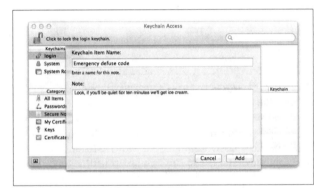

Figure 7-3. They must never know

Add a Keychain Access Menu Extra

With all the goodness Keychain Access offers, you might want easy access to it. You can add it to your Dock, but that might be getting a little crowded, and the Keychain icon isn't the best-looking one Apple has churned out. Luckily, you can add a menu extra for Keychain Access (see "Menu extras" on page 53 for a refresher). To do that, the next time you're using Keychain Access, go to Preferences (⌘-,) and, on the General tab, check the box next to "Show keychain status in menu bar."

Securing Your Data

Carefully choosing passwords is a great start when it comes to security, but it's not a perfect solution. If someone has physical access to your Mac, there are things she can do to get at your data. If this prospect seems particularly loathsome to you, consider making the extra effort to enable FileVault, a feature of Mountain Lion that makes your data impossible to access unless you want it accessed. For information on setting up FileVault, see "FileVault tab" on page 131.

CHAPTER 8

Keyboard Commands and Special Characters

When you're using the keyboard, you want to keep your hands on the keys. A trip to the trackpad, reaching for the mouse, or hunting for a special character can really slow you down. The good news is that Mountain Lion has a lot of key commands and special characters built right in. The bad news is that, unless you're one of those people who memorize the digits of pi to a thousand places for fun, you won't remember them all.

The most important key commands and special characters vary from user to user. For example, if you're writing about Exposé, knowing how to type é really helps, but knowing how to type ¬ isn't of much use. Everyone uses his or her Mac a little differently, so this chapter features a wide selection of keyboard commands and ways to type different characters. Memorize the ones for the functions you use most, and you'll save a lot of time and effort.

Key Commands

When your hands are on the keyboard, it's much quicker to keep them there to perform some mundane task than it is to dig through the menus and find the option that lets you type a special character or create a new folder.

In general, the less time you spend using the mouse (or trackpad), the more productive you'll be. While you'll want to learn the keyboard commands for all your favorite programs, some commands are so common that it's worth reserving a special spot for them in your brain:

⌘-S

> Save. This saves the document you're working on. The more often you use this command, the happier you'll be (at least until OS X's Auto Save feature is part of every program). Nothing is more frustrating than having all your hard work disappear when the power flickers or an application crashes.

NOTE

If you're using a keyboard designed for Windows systems, you won't see the ⌘ key. Instead, use the Windows key, which is usually in the same spot you'd find the ⌘ key. Some keyboards use a different symbol, however; for example, the Happy Hacking Keyboard uses the "lozenge" symbol (◊).

⌘-C

> Copy. This command copies the current selection for later pasting.

⌘-X

> Cut. This command deletes the current selection but copies it to your Mac's memory. After you've cut something, you can paste it elsewhere (until you copy or cut something else, that is).

⌘-V

> Paste. Once you've copied or cut something, you'll want to paste it.

⌘-,

    Opens the preferences for the active application.

⌘-] *and* ⌘-[

    Moves forward (]) or backward ([) in the Finder, Safari, and some other applications. For example, when navigating to various directories in the Finder, you can use these keys instead of clicking the arrows in the upper-right corner of the window.

⌘-Shift-?

    Opens the current application's Help dialog box so you can get quick answers to your vexing questions.

⌘-Q

    Quits the current application.

NOTE

You can't easily quit the Finder, so this command doesn't work when you're using it. To find out how to quit the Finder (or more accurately, relaunch it), see "The Finder stops responding" on page 105.

⌘-Tab

    Brings up the Application Switcher, which lets you cycle through running applications by pressing Tab repeatedly as you hold down ⌘. When you get to the application you're after, let go of both keys. If your hands are on the keyboard, this is a *much* faster way to switch applications than the Dock.

Option-⌘-*Esc*

    Force quits the current program.

Once you've mastered those commands, your appetite for keyboard shortcuts is likely to become insatiable. Fortunately, there's plenty more of that keyboard-shortcut, time-saving goodness, much of which is shown in Table 8-1.

NOTE

Unfortunately, some of these commands don't work the same way in all programs. For example, in the Finder and many other applications, ⌘-I displays the Get Info window for the currently selected file or object, but in most word-processing applications, ⌘-I italicizes the selected text.

Also, on some keyboards, you may need to hold down the key labeled Fn to use keyboard shortcuts that require a function key (F1, F2, etc.).

Table 8-1. Common keyboard shortcuts

Key command	Most common action	Finder action
⌘-A	Selects all	Selects all items in current directory
⌘-B	Makes selected text bold (in word-processing programs)	None
⌘-C	Copies current selection	Copies selected files and folders
⌘-D	Duplicates selected object (usually in drawing applications)	Duplicates selected file or folder
⌘-E	Searches for highlighted text	Ejects disk
⌘-F	Finds text	Opens a new Finder window with cursor in search field
⌘-H	Hides current application	Hides Finder
⌘-I	Italicizes selected text	Opens Get Info window for selected item
⌘-J	Jumps to currently selected text (useful if you've selected some text, then scrolled elsewhere in a document)	Shows View options
⌘-K	Clears screen (Terminal) or inserts hyperlink (text editors, word processors, and Mail)	Opens "Connect to Server" window

Key command	Most common action	Finder action
⌘-L	Opens dialog box that lets you jump to a specific line of text (common in text editors)	Creates an alias
⌘-M	Minimizes window	Minimizes window
⌘-N	Creates new document	Opens new Finder window
⌘-O	Displays Open File dialog box	Opens selected item
⌘-P	Prints	None
⌘-Q	Quits current application	None
⌘-R	Varies	Shows original file when an alias is selected
⌘-S	Saves current file	None
⌘-T	Displays Font panel	Adds selected item to Finder window sidebar
⌘-V	Pastes copied item	Pastes copied file(s) or folder(s)
⌘-W	Closes window	Closes window
⌘-X	Cuts	None
⌘-Z	Undoes most recent action	Undoes most recent action
⌘-1	Varies	Displays Finder items as icons
⌘-2	Varies	Displays Finder items as list
⌘-3	Varies	Displays Finder items as columns
⌘-4	Varies	Displays Finder items in Cover Flow View
⌘-Delete	Varies	Moves selected item to Trash
⌘-Tab	Opens Application Switcher	Opens Application Switcher
⌘-[	Goes back one page (in web browsers)	Goes back one directory
⌘-]	Goes forward one page (in web browsers)	Goes forward one directory
⌘-?	Activates Help menu	Activates Help menu
⌘-space bar	Activates Spotlight search	Activates Spotlight search

Key command	Most common action	Finder action
⌘-'	Cycles through application windows	Cycles through Finder windows
Tab	Moves focus to next item or (in text editors) inserts a tab	Moves focus to next item
Shift-⌘-3	Takes a picture of your screen; saves image file to desktop	Takes a picture of your screen; saves image file to desktop
Shift-⌘-4	Displays a cursor for taking a snapshot of part of the screen (to take a picture of a single window, press space bar after using this keyboard shortcut); saves image file to desktop	Displays a cursor for taking a snapshot of part of the screen (to take a picture of a single window, press space bar after using this keyboard shortcut); saves image file to desktop
Shift-Control-⌘-3	Works like ⌘-Shift-3, but copies picture to Clipboard	Works like ⌘-Shift-3, but copies picture to Clipboard
Shift-Control-⌘-4	Works like ⌘-Shift-4, but copies picture to Clipboard	Works like ⌘-Shift-4, but copies picture to Clipboard
Shift-⌘-A	Varies	Opens Applications folder
Shift-⌘-C	Varies	Opens Computer folder
Shift-⌘-D	Varies	Opens Desktop folder
Shift-⌘-O	Varies	Opens Documents folder
Shift-⌘-G	Varies	Opens "Go to the folder" dialog box
Shift-⌘-H	Varies	Opens Home folder
Shift-⌘-K	Varies	Opens Network folder
Shift-⌘-N	Varies	Creates a new folder
Shift-⌘-Q	Displays logout dialog box, logs out automatically after one minute	Displays logout dialog box, logs out automatically after one minute
Shift-⌘-S	Opens "Save As..." dialog box	None
Shift-⌘-U	Varies	Opens Utilities folder
Shift-⌘-Delete	Varies	Opens Empty Trash dialog box

Key command	Most common action	Finder action
Shift-Option-⌘-Delete	Varies	Empties Trash
Option (while dragging)	Copies item to new location	Copies file/folder to new location
⌘-Option (while dragging)	Varies	Creates an alias to a file/folder at new location
Option-⌘-D	Shows/hides the Dock	Shows/hides the Dock
Option-⌘-M	Varies	Minimizes all windows
Option-⌘-Esc	Opens a dialog box that allows you to force quit an app	Opens a dialog box that allows you to force quit an app
Option-⌘-Eject	Puts computer to sleep	Puts computer to sleep
Control-Eject	Displays the Restart/Sleep/Shut Down dialog box	Displays the Restart/Sleep/Shut Down dialog box
Control-⌘-Eject	Quits all applications and restarts computer	Quits all applications and restarts computer

You're probably not going to remember *all* those shortcuts, but you'll likely remember the ones you use frequently. And more time at the keyboard means less time wasted mousing and searching for commands.

Customizing Key Commands

If you don't like the key commands built into OS X, you don't have to put up with them. You can change them or add your own by taking a trip to the Keyboard preference pane. For details, see "Keyboard" on page 139.

Typing Special Characters in OS X

If you're banging away on the keyboard and find yourself wanting to type special characters (like the é in Exposé, for example), there are convoluted methods of getting the character you want (pasting them from the Web, say). But you might be wondering if there's a trackpadless or mouse-free way to do it. Fortunately, there is.

In OS X Lion, Apple added an easy way to get at those pesky diacritical symbols. Simply type the letter you're interested in and *hold the key down*; a window will pop up with all your options (as in Figure 8-1). You can then use the arrow keys to select the diacritic, click the one you want, or press the number key that corresponds to the number below your pick.

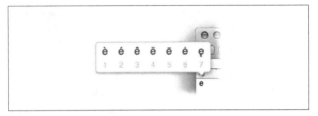

Figure 8-1. All your options for e

This feature is universal, so you can use it anywhere you can type a character. It does have a couple of drawbacks, though: depending on how your key repeat rate is set (see "Keyboard" on page 139), you might find yourself typing *sss* before the diacritic menu shows up; and if you type a special character often, it's faster to commit its keyboard shortcut to memory instead. Table 8-2 shows how to easily type diacritical symbols.

Table 8-2. Diacritical accent mark shortcuts

Symbol	Name	Keystroke
´	Acute	Option-E, then type the letter
∧	Circumflex	Option-I, then type the letter
`	Grave	Option-`, then type the letter
~	Tilde	Option-N, then type the letter
¨	Umlaut	Option-U, then type the letter

That takes care of only a few characters you may not be able to find on your keyboard. But what about other characters, such as the euro symbol or the Apple logo? You might try looking through the Font Book utility, but with the number of fonts included in a standard OS X install, that task can require more luck than skill.

The Character Palette is a bit easier to use. You enable it by heading to →System Preferences→Language & Text. Click the Input Sources tab, and then check the box labeled Keyboard & Character Viewer. Your Mac adds a new icon to the menu bar that lets you launch either Character Viewer or Keyboard Viewer. Character Viewer lets you browse a wide variety of special characters and insert them into documents by clicking them (the characters appear in the most recently used application). With Keyboard Viewer (Figure 8-2), you can hold down Shift, Option, or Shift *and* Option simultaneously to see how the keyboard is modified when you're depressing those modifier keys. As with Character Viewer, simply click a letter or a symbol to insert it into a text field.

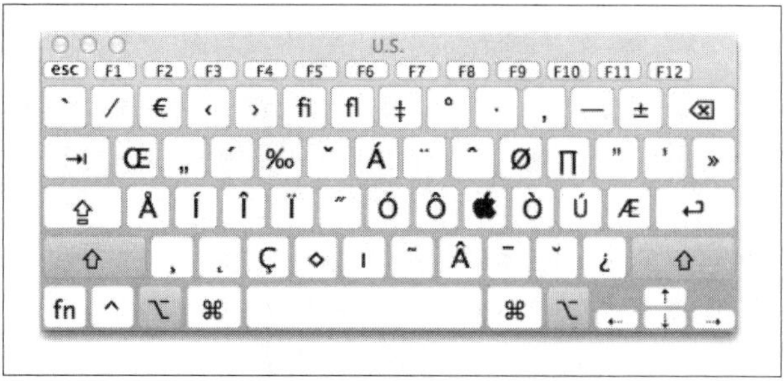

Figure 8-2. Wonder what Option-Shift does to the characters on your keyboard? Wonder no more!

You can also check out Table 8-3 for a quick reference to U.S. English keyboard modifiers.

Table 8-3. Special character shortcuts for U.S. English keyboards

No modifiers	Shift	Option	Shift-Option
`	~	` (above next vowel typed)	`
1	!	¡	⁄ (fraction slash symbol)
2	@	™	Œ
3	#	£	‹
4	$	¢	›
5	%	∞	fi (ligature)
6	^	§	fl (ligature)
7	&	¶	‡
8	*	•	°
9	(	ª	·
0	)	º	‚
-	–	–	—
=	+	≠	±
q	Q	Œ	Œ
w	W	Σ	„
e	E	´ (above next vowel typed)	´
r	R	®	‰
t	T	†	ˇ
y	Y	¥	Á
u	U	¨ (above next vowel typed)	¨
i	I	^ (above next vowel typed)	^
o	O	ø	Ø
p	P	π	∏
[	{	"	"
]	}	'	'
\	|	«	»
a	A	å	Å
s	S	ß	Í

No modifiers	Shift	Option	Shift-Option
d	D	∂	Î
f	F	ƒ	Ï
g	G	©	"
h	H	·	Ó
j	J	Δ	Ô
k	K	°	
l	L	¬	Ò
;	:	…	Ú
'	"	Æ	Æ
z	Z	Ω	¸
x	X	≈	˛
c	C	Ç	Ç
v	V	√	◊
b	B	∫	ı
n	N	~ (above next "n" typed)	˜
m	M	µ	Â
,	<	≤	¯
.	>	≥	˘
/	?	÷	¿

Index

Symbols

We'd like to hear your suggestions for improving our indexes. Send email to *index@oreilly.com*.

About the Author

Chris Seibold is an engineer, writer, and cartoonist residing in Knoxville, Tennessee. As an engineer, he has tackled such diverse processes as powder coating and hot dog casing manufacture. As a writer, he has focused on computing and written for a variety of online and traditional media, including serving as senior contributing editor for the Apple Matters website and contributing hacks to iPod and iTunes Hacks, with a talent for making the complex accessible to the interested but harried user. As a cartoonist, he has produced both cartoon strips and editorials. Chris also managed to spend some time producing radio shows relating to sports. As soon as he hits television, the trifecta will be complete. Chris lives with his wife, young son, and what is quite possibly the world's dimmest canine. He has a degree in physics from the University of Tennessee but has yet to find work involving frictionless inclined planes.

Colophon

The animal on the cover of *OS X Mountain Lion Pocket Guide* is a puma (*Puma concolor*). The puma is known by varying names in different regions, including mountain lion, mountain cat, catamount, or panther. This mammal of the family Felidae is native to the Americas. Only trumped in size by the jaguar, the puma is the second heaviest cat in the Western Hemisphere, where it also boasts the largest range of any large wild terrestrial mammal. Pumas can be found in any major American habitat stretching from Canada to South America.

The puma is known for its stalk-and-ambush style of hunting, and feeds on wild animals—elk, deer, moose, bighorn sheep—as well as domestic animals such as horses, sheep, and cattle. These cats prefer habitats that lend to stalking, such as dense brush and rocky areas. The puma's major competitors for prey include the grey wolf, American black bear, jaguar, and the grizzly bear.

Excessive hunting and human development has caused population numbers to drop in recent years, and populations of pumas have recently begun to move east into parts of the Midwest, including the Dakotas, Nebraska, and Oklahoma.

The cover image is from *Lydekker's Royal Natural History*. The cover font is Adobe ITC Garamond. The text font is Linotype Birka; the heading font is Adobe Myriad Condensed; and the code font is LucasFont's TheSansMonoCondensed.

The information you need, when and where you need it.

With Safari Books Online, you can:

Access the contents of thousands of technology and business books

- Quickly search over 7000 books and certification guides
- Download whole books or chapters in PDF format, at no extra cost, to print or read on the go
- Copy and paste code
- Save up to 35% on O'Reilly print books
- **New!** Access mobile-friendly books directly from cell phones and mobile devices

Stay up-to-date on emerging topics before the books are published

- Get on-demand access to evolving manuscripts.
- Interact directly with authors of upcoming books

Explore thousands of hours of video on technology and design topics

- Learn from expert video tutorials
- Watch and replay recorded conference sessions

O'REILLY®

Spreading the knowledge of innovators   oreilly.com

©2011 O'Reilly Media, Inc. O'Reilly logo is a registered trademark of O'Reilly Media, Inc. 00000

Get even more for your money.

Join the O'Reilly Community, and register the O'Reilly books you own. It's free, and you'll get:

- $4.99 ebook upgrade offer
- 40% upgrade offer on O'Reilly print books
- Membership discounts on books and events
- Free lifetime updates to ebooks and videos
- Multiple ebook formats, DRM FREE
- Participation in the O'Reilly community
- Newsletters
- Account management
- 100% Satisfaction Guarantee

Registering your books is easy:

1. Go to: oreilly.com/go/register
2. Create an O'Reilly login.
3. Provide your address.
4. Register your books.

Note: English-language books only

To order books online:
oreilly.com/store

For questions about products or an order:
orders@oreilly.com

To sign up to get topic-specific email announcements and/or news about upcoming books, conferences, special offers, and new technologies:
elists@oreilly.com

For technical questions about book content:
booktech@oreilly.com

To submit new book proposals to our editors:
proposals@oreilly.com

O'Reilly books are available in multiple DRM-free ebook formats. For more information:
oreilly.com/ebooks

O'REILLY®

Spreading the knowledge of innovators   oreilly.com

©2010 O'Reilly Media, Inc. O'Reilly logo is a registered trademark of O'Reilly Media, Inc. 00000